CAMBRIDGE LIBRARY COLLECTION

Books of enduring scholarly value

Religion

For centuries, scripture and theology were the focus of prodigious amounts of scholarship and publishing, dominated in the English-speaking world by the work of Protestant Christians. Enlightenment philosophy and science, anthropology, ethnology and the colonial experience all brought new perspectives, lively debates and heated controversies to the study of religion and its role in the world, many of which continue to this day. This series explores the editing and interpretation of religious texts, the history of religious ideas and institutions, and not least the encounter between religion and science.

The Religious Aspect of Evolution

The Scottish scholar James McCosh (1811-94) was a champion of the Free church, a successful and much-published philosophy professor at Belfast for 16 years, and an energetic and innovative President of Princeton University from 1868 to 1888. *The Religious Aspect of Evolution* was published in 1888, and this second edition from 1890 took account of A. R. Wallace's latest work, *Darwinism* (1889, also reissued in this series). McCosh, who already in Ireland had developed a 'theory of the universe conditioned by Christian revelation' was one of very few clergymen in America who defended evolutionary theory and insisted that, if properly understood, far from denying the existence of God it increased the reader's wonder at the mystery of creation. He impressed upon his students that while there seemed to be great truth in Darwin's theory, there was also error in the common expositions surrounding it, and that the work of the coming age must be to separate the truth from the error. In doing so, McCosh claimed, illustrations of God's existence would be found as it relates to the origins of species, thus enabling scholars to follow and even embrace science while also retaining their faith in the Bible.

Cambridge University Press has long been a pioneer in the reissuing of out-of-print titles from its own backlist, producing digital reprints of books that are still sought after by scholars and students but could not be reprinted economically using traditional technology. The Cambridge Library Collection extends this activity to a wider range of books which are still of importance to researchers and professionals, either for the source material they contain, or as landmarks in the history of their academic discipline.

Drawing from the world-renowned collections in the Cambridge University Library, and guided by the advice of experts in each subject area, Cambridge University Press is using state-of-the-art scanning machines in its own Printing House to capture the content of each book selected for inclusion. The files are processed to give a consistently clear, crisp image, and the books finished to the high quality standard for which the Press is recognised around the world. The latest print-on-demand technology ensures that the books will remain available indefinitely, and that orders for single or multiple copies can quickly be supplied.

The Cambridge Library Collection will bring back to life books of enduring scholarly value (including out-of-copyright works originally issued by other publishers) across a wide range of disciplines in the humanities and social sciences and in science and technology.

The Religious Aspect of Evolution

JAMES McCOSH

CAMBRIDGE
UNIVERSITY PRESS

CAMBRIDGE UNIVERSITY PRESS

Cambridge, New York, Melbourne, Madrid, Cape Town, Singapore,
São Paolo, Delhi, Dubai, Tokyo, Mexico City

Published in the United States of America by Cambridge University Press, New York

www.cambridge.org
Information on this title: www.cambridge.org/9781108000161

© in this compilation Cambridge University Press 2010

This edition first published 1890
This digitally printed version 2010

ISBN 978-1-108-00016-1 Paperback

THE RELIGIOUS ASPECT
OF EVOLUTION.

DR. McCOSH'S WORKS.

FIRST AND FUNDAMENTAL TRUTHS. Being a Treatise on Meta-
physics.

PSYCHOLOGY. The Cognitive Powers.

PSYCHOLOGY. The Motive Powers.

THE EMOTIONS.

REALISTIC PHILOSOPHY. Defended in a Philosophic Series. 2 vols.,
12mo. Vol. I., Expository. Vol. II., Historical and Critical.

THE NEW DEPARTURE IN COLLEGE EDUCATION.

WHITHER? O WHITHER?

THE METHOD OF THE DIVINE GOVERNMENT. Physical and
Moral.

TYPICAL FORMS AND SPECIAL ENDS IN CREATION.

THE INTUITIONS OF THE MIND.

A DEFENCE OF FUNDAMENTAL TRUTH.

SCOTTISH PHILOSOPHY. Biographical, Expository, and Critical.

LAWS OF DISCURSIVE THOUGHT, CHRISTIANITY, AND POSITIVISM.

THE RELIGIOUS ASPECT

OF

EVOLUTION

BY

JAMES McCOSH, D.D., LL.D., Litt.D.

Ex-President of Princeton College

AUTHOR OF "METHOD OF DIVINE GOVERNMENT"; "REALISTIC PHILOSOPHY";
"PSYCHOLOGY—THE COGNITIVE POWERS"; "PSYCHOLOGY—THE MOTIVE
POWERS"; "FIRST AND FUNDAMENTAL TRUTHS"; "TESTS
OF VARIOUS KINDS OF TRUTH."

ENLARGED AND IMPROVED EDITION

LONDON

JAMES NISBET & CO.

21, BERNERS STREET

PREFATORY NOTE TO SECOND EDITION.

THIS work was first published as one of the Bedell Lectures, founded by the Rev. Dr. Bedell, Bishop of Ohio, and Mrs. Bedell. In issuing this second edition in a somewhat different form, I have inserted a chapter on " Final Cause," and used materials from Dr. A. R. Wallace's recently published work on " Darwinism."

PREFACE.

In my first published work, " The Method of Divine Government," I sought to unfold the plan by which God governs the world, and I found it to be in an orderly manner—that is, by law. As having pursued this line of research, I was prepared to believe that there might be the like method in the organic kingdoms, and to listen to Darwin when he showed that there was a regular instrumentality in the descent of plants and animals. I noticed that he and others, such as Lewes, Huxley, and Spencer, who took the same view, were not swayed by any religious considerations, and that religious people generally were strongly prepossessed against the new doctrine. But I saw, at the same time, that Darwin was a most careful observer, that he published many important facts, that there was great truth in the theory, and that there was nothing atheistic in it if properly understood—that is, in the ac-

knowledged tenet of the government of organic nature by means and according to law.

I felt it to be my only course not to reject
the truth because it was proclaimed by some
who turned it to an irreligious use, but to ac-
cept it wherever it might lead, and to turn it
to a better use. I let it be known that while
I thought there was truth, I believed there
was error in the common expositions of evolution, and that the work of the coming age
must be to separate the truth from the error,
when it would be found, I was sure, that this,
like every other part of God's work, would
illustrate his existence and his wisdom.

When I was called from the Old World to
the office which I now hold as president of an
important college, I had to consider—I remember seriously pondering the question in
the vessel which brought me to this country—
whether I should at once avow my convictions
or keep them in abeyance because of the preju-
dices of religious men, and lest I might un-
settle the faith of the students committed to
my care. I decided to pursue the open and
honest course, as being sure that it would be the
best in the end. I was not a week in Princeton till I let it be known to the upper classes

of the college that I was in favor of evolution properly limited and explained ; and I have proclaimed my views in lectures and papers in a number of cities and before various associations, literary and religious. I have been gratified to find that none of the churches has assailed me, and this has convinced me that their doubts about evolution have proceeded mainly from the bad use to which the doctrine has been turned. I am pleased to discover that intelligent Christians are coming round gradually to the views which I have had the courage to publish.

I have all along had a sensitive apprehension that the undiscriminating denunciation of evolution from so many pulpits, periodicals, and seminaries might drive some of our thoughtful young men to infidelity, as they clearly saw development everywhere in nature, and were at the same time told by their advisers that they could not believe in evolution and yet be Christians. I am gratified beyond measure to find that I am thanked by my pupils, some of whom have reached the highest position as naturalists, because in showing them evolution in the works of God, I showed them that this was not inconsistent with reli-

gion, and thus enabled them to follow science
and yet retain their faith in the Bible.[1]

[1] As I am a mere amateur naturalist (at one time a very enthusi-
astic one) I have laid these papers before my former pupils, now emi-
nent naturalists, Dr. Macloskie, Professor of Natural History, Dr.
Scott, Professor of Geology, Dr. Osborn, Professor of Comparative
Anatomy, in Princeton College, and accepted their corrections. I
have made use of the able works of Dana, LeConte, and Geikie on
geology ; also of Dawson's "Story of the Earth and Man," of
Cope's "Origin of the Fittest," of Conn's "Evolution of To-day,"
and of Wallace's "Darwinism."

CONTENTS.

CHAPTER I.

I.

EVOLUTION AND CAUSATION.—Evolution, the drawing of one thing out of another, is deep in nature. It proceeds from causation, which is universal. In the world things are so connected that every one thing proceeds from some other, and all things from God. This arises from the universal action of causation. A cause (in physical nature) develops into an effect, and an effect is an evolution from a cause. The All-Mighty God, in all his works, might have acted immediately—that is, without any creature instrumentality. He might have produced crops and cattle, heaved up mountains and lowered plains, determined birth and death without the use of means of any kind. But in this case I do not see how mankind, with their present faculties, could have anticipated any of these occurrences, as it is only by the preparations for them that we

1

know that they are coming. God has been pleased to arrange instead that every physical event has a physical cause,—the only exception being the miracles of the Old and New Testaments, which serve their purpose because they are exceptions. Causation is universal in physical nature, and causation develops all we see, or, to express it otherwise, all that we see is evolved from causes. We shall see that the evolution of plants and animals is produced by organized causes.

II.

NATURE OF CAUSATION.—I do not mean to enter into the deep discussions on this subject. We know a little more of causation in these later years. All natural causation is produced by two or more bodies acting on each other, the effect being that both are changed. A ball in motion strikes a ball at rest ; this constitutes the cause, and the effect is that the ball in motion is stayed, and the ball at rest moves, the two constituting the effect. It has to be added that heat is produced by the impact, being part of the effect. A stone strikes a board ; this is the cause, and the effect is the stone arrested in its course and the board broken. Cold air blows on a living plant; this is the cause, and the effect is the temperature of the air insensibly affected and the plant killed. Causes always consist of two or more agents called con-causes; effects consist of the same agents changed. The effects, which are also dual or plural, are ready with other agents to act as causes. Nature thus becomes reticulated and flexible. The evolution of living beings is an organized causation.

III.

DEVELOPMENT IN NATURE. —Suppose that nature, as created by God at the beginning, consists of a hundred or a thousand agents. These act upon each other according to their properties, and new products are ever appearing. There can be no impropriety in saying that they are evolved from their antecedents, which have the power of developing them. A complex effect is the evolution of a complexity of causes—say the downfall of the Roman empire, or the Renaissance of the fifteenth century. Such is God's method of distributing causes throughout the cosmos. It is our business not to rebel against the plan, but to fall in with it and profit by it. We can so far see its beneficial tendency. Looking to the causes operating, we can from the present so far find out the past and forecast the future. We can take advantage of these causes and combinations of causes to develop the results, general and special, which we wish to accomplish. Limited though our view be, we can see that the method is worthy of God, and suited to the intelligence of man. We sow in spring because we know that the seed will produce fruit in harvest.

We are all familiar with organic development, though we may not have been giving it this formidable name. We are privileged to be descended from parents. Of mature age, I know that I am developed from the boy of six as I remember him going to school. Our horses, our cattle, and dogs are of a breed which can be determined. The bread we eat sprang from seed. We do not complain of these evolutions; we do not denounce them as atheistic. We are grateful for some of them; as, for example, that we have been nursed by a mother's love and watched over by a father's care. The new evolutions of plants and animal races which we are now called to consider, may only be a farther evolution of the old ones. Possibly the one set

may be no more atheistic than the others.
Both may be illustrations of Divine method,
of which we can so far see the wisdom.

IV.

THE QUESTION BETWEEN EVOLUTIONISTS
AND NON-EVOLUTIONISTS.—" No man can find
out the work that God maketh from the beginning to the end." But though human science
cannot go back to the beginning nor go on to
the end, and while there is much in the middle
that is concealed, there are whole provinces
which we can inquire into and come to know.
"We know in part." We now know not a
little about the generation of our earth, and of
the plants and animals upon its surface. And
we can tell much about the order in which
animated beings appeared. But there is a
keen dispute as to how they were produced.

All admit that there is system in the production of the organic world. Those who have no
faith in a power above nature, ascribe it to
physical forces. Religious people, so far from
denying this, should at once admit and pro-
claim it ; and seek to find out what the forces
are and the laws they follow. We cannot
allow God to be separated from his works, and
so we must resolutely hold that God is in the

forces arranged into an order—that is, laws, which we find it so interesting to observe.

But this is not just the burning question of the day. There is a perplexing confusion in the statement of the question. It has been misunderstood by religious, it has been perverted by irreligious, people. The former often speak of it as being : Whether all things are to be ascribed to God, or a portion to God, while the rest is handed over to material agency? In maintaining this latter view they furnish an excuse or pretext to those who would ascribe the descent of plants and animals to mechanical agency. The great body of naturalists, all younger than forty, certainly all younger than thirty, are sure that they see evolution in nature ; but they are assured by their teachers or the religious press that, if evolution does every thing, there is nothing left for God to do, and they see no proof of his existence. Many a youth is brought to a crisis in his belief and life by such a representation. He feels that he must give up either his science or his faith, and his head is distracted, and his heart is tortured till feelings more bitter than tears are wrung from it.

The question is said to be, Whether the

origin of species and descent of living creatures
are by supernatural power or natural law, by
Creator or creative action, by design or by
mechanism, by contrivance or by chance, by
purpose or without purpose.

Mr. Darwin, followed by Dr. Romanes, and
many others, is constantly drawing the distinction in this form : between "natural selection" and "supernatural design," between
"natural law" and "special creation." Now
the difference between the two opposing theo-
ries as thus put is misleading, and this whether
put by disbelief or by belief. The supernatural
power is to be recognized in the natural law.
The Creator's power is executed by creature
action. The design is seen in the mechanism.
Chance is obliged to vanish because we see
contrivance. There is purpose when we see
a beneficent end accomplished. Supernatural
design produces natural selection. Special
creation is included in universal creation.

A question is often settled by being properly
stated. The *status quæstionis*, as the scholas-
tics expressed it, is here not between God and
not-God, but between God working without
means and by means, the means being created
by God and working for him. There may be

evidence of design, of contrivance, and purpose
in the very means employed.   If an optician
brings me a microscope I have only to examine
it to discover design in it, but I may have as
clear proof of purpose when I visit his shop
and see him manufacturing the instrument.
There is nothing atheistic in the creed that
God proceeds by instruments, which we may
find to be for the good of his creatures.   There
may be a want of reverence toward God and
truth when there is evidence laid before us in
its favor and we refuse to look at it.   I should
discover God in the human frame, on the supposition that he created it at once, but I have
quite as satisfactory evidence on the supposition that he produced it by a father and mother,
and provided that it should grow to maturity
by a natural process.   In the geological development I am privileged as it were to enter
God's workshop and see his modes of operation, and the result reached so full of provisions
in bones, muscles, joints, for the good of the
creature.

V.

TENDENCY OF A SET OF CAUSES TO DIFFER-
ENTIATE AND INTEGRATE.—Our cosmic system
consists of a number of elements, supposed at

present to be seventy, and of the properties
possessed by them, such as gravitating, mechanical, and chemical power ; these with an
order or collocation imposed on them by God
at the beginning.   As they begin to act, which
they do by their very nature as imparted to
them by God, they differentiate.   Things con-
joined separate, complexities being dissolved
by some of the composites having greater affin-
ities to other things.   There commence at the
same time integrations ; and new combinations are formed by gravitation, by chemical
affinity, and other powers.   These two processes are continually going on.   At last, however, many integrations become fixed, so that
they never change.   Some have supposed that
carbon is not an element, but a compound
which cannot be dissolved in ordinary circumstances.   Thus sea and land are distributed,
mountains and rocks are formed, lakes and
rivers are spread out.   If organisms are ruled,
as they undoubtedly are, by the law of cause
and effect, there must be a like variation and
conservation in their actions.

VI.

UNIFORMITY WITH VARIATIONS IN ORGAN-
ISMS.—Plants and animals are the result of

combinations, being composed of oxygen, hydrogen, carbon, and nitrogen, the elements which form the most stable combinations, with a few others not so universally present. These are made, always by the power of God, to differentiate and combine into divisions, which are appropriately called Kinds. There are classes which are entitled to be called Natural; such, for example, is the division into fishes, amphibians, reptiles, birds, and mammals. The resemblance in the objects in the Kind is produced by their being of the same composition, but mainly from their being descended from a seed or germ which is a concentrated combination of powers. While there is a sameness there is also a variation. This may be produced by the mutual action of the elements within the organism itself. It is thus, for example, that old age and death are brought upon living beings. But the most conspicuous agent is what is called Environment. Every object has surroundings which act upon it. A fertile soil makes a plant grow and expand, while a barren soil dwarfs it.

VII.

CLASSIFICATION BY RAMIFICATION.—The classification of organisms is not now made as it used to be—by concentric circles within circles, genera within orders, and species within genera—but rather by ramification, with trunk and branches, branchlets, twigs, and leaves. So in the vegetable and animal systems we have common stock, and proceeding from it SUB-KINGDOMS, CLASSES, FAMILIES, ORDERS, GENERA, and SPECIES. This is the common division now of the vegetable and animal kingdoms. It shows us one system with means to produce it. Since the days of Aristotle, plants and animals have been classified according to type. It is thus that the great Cuvier has arranged the animal kingdom. The types have been fondly contemplated and admired by our profounder minds. They have been identified with the grand Ideas which, according to Plato, have been in or before the Divine mind from all eternity. Pious minds in modern times have ascribed them to God, whose thoughts are embodied in them. On the other hand the great rival of Cuvier, St. Hilaire, ascribed the types to a common descent, and used language which sounded as if the animal, by its wishes, could add to its organs ; could call forth fins to swim with, and wings to fly. The controversy came to a head in 1830, when Goethe declared that it was of

more importance than the French Revolution,
which was at that time ringing in the ears of
Europe. There is undoubtedly a difference
between the two views ; but may there not be
a reconciliation ? It may be by descent that
types are formed, and yet all be done by a plan
in the Divine wisdom which is thus manifested.
The two great Swiss-American naturalists,
Agassiz and Guyot, delighted to perceive
clearly that there was a system in the descent
of animals which they were sure was conceived
in the Divine mind, but doubted whether it
could have been produced by natural law or
material agency.   But surely, in analogy with
the Divine procedure in all other parts of nature, we may discover a Divine plan, and at
the same time a creature agency to carry it
out, which agency makes known God's plan to
us.   We may see that the relations which constitute types are genetic, and as we perceive in
them wisdom and beauty, we can also perceive
that they are instituted by God.   This view
gives to classes a connection in the very nature
of things, and makes species intelligible to human intelligence, which thereby rises to some
comprehension of Divine intelligence, in the
image of which human intelligence is formed.

VIII.

CONTINUANCE AND DISAPPEARANCE OF SPE-
CIES.—In some cases the genera and species of
plants and animals are unchanged for thousands or even millions of years. As instances
we may mention the Trilobites, which appear in
the Cambrian and remain till the Carboniferous epoch, when they disappear. The small
bivalve shell, the Lingula, and the Nautilus
can be traced back in a line to the earliest
animal ages. So can some of the earthworms
which have been busy in forming a soil for us.
We may point also to the Ferns which present
themselves in the Old Red Sandstone and the
Coal Measures, and adorn our fields and up-
lands at this day. The fossil scorpions, found
in Scotland and Gothland, are the same as
those of our day. As illustrations of a different kind of the same continuance, we may refer to the figures of negroes on the monuments
of Egypt, identical with the forms of the same
race at the present day. Mr. Carruthers tells
us that the leaves of grape vines found in the
Egyptian tombs are identical with those of our
time. We may also mention the Chinese, the
same in the color of their skin, their language,
tastes, and habits since they first appeared in

history. All this is easily accounted for. The animated beings have lived in scenes in which they have not been disturbed by their surroundings.

In other cases the plants and animals have undergone a series of changes. We may illustrate this by the history of the horse tribe. The earliest form is found in the Eocene rocks, where it treads the often soft ground with five toes, the typical number. Next it appears with three toes on the hind foot, and four perfect serviceable toes on the fore foot, with imperfect splint bones in the fore foot, and apparently a dew-claw on the hind foot. It is then about the size of a fox. Next comes the Orohippus, with the dew-claw dropped. Then we have in the lower Miocene the Mesohippus, in which the fourth toe has become a splint. Next the Miohippus, with the splint nearly gone, and the middle hoof larger. The animal is now about the size of a sheep. After this is the Protohippus in the upper Miocene and lower Pliocene, now about the size of an ass, with the middle toe larger and the two side hoofs shorter. The animal is becoming more and more like the modern horse. In the Pliocene we have the

Equus, almost a complete horse, with the hoofs reduced to one, the splints of the two sides remaining to attest the descent. Finally, in the human period, the Equus Caballus, our horse, perhaps the most elegant and useful to man of all animals, with the hoofs rounder and the second bone of the leg more rudimentary, and the splint bones shortened, still remaining. From the normal number of five, the toes have been successively dropped according to a regular law—first, the thumb, No. 1 ; then the little finger, No. 5 ; then the index, No. 2 ; same time the ring-finger, No. 4 ; and the middle finger, No. 3, only remains.[1] This is an apposite example of the way in which, by a process, God has provided the horse with its hard hoof for man, who to make it harder adds a shoe. I hold that there are as clear proofs of design in the hoof as in the shoe upon it.

IX.

CAUSES OF VARIATION.—The main cause is the tendency of complex bodies to differentiate. See p. 8. But there are special agencies. (1) I may mention the one to which Darwin has given such prominence. It is that of "Natural Selection," not a very happy phrase, as it

[1] Le Conte's " Elementary Geology," page 509.

is apt to leave the impression that there is
a choice on the part of nature, whereas it is
all produced by the arrangements made by the
Creator.   This law is otherwise called the
" Survival of the Fittest."   This principle is
undoubtedly operating in all organic nature,
and has mighty influences, as, for instance, in
the five loose toes becoming one solid hoof in
the horse.   A tree, say an oak, expands in an
English nobleman's park, where it has a rich
soil and room to breathe in, and is dwarfed or
dies in a cold and stormy climate.   The rose
grows into greatest fulness and becomes the La
France in a cultivated garden.   The principle
of the survival of the fittest is a beneficent provision, as it preserves the strong and the useful, while the weak is allowed to die out and
leave room for something else to take its place
in the exuberance of God's works.   The religious man should not object to it, if at certain
junctures it produces a newer and higher
species of plant or animal to make up, it may be,
for the disappearance of an old species, say, of
a mammal instead of a reptile.

(2) There is the strength produced by the
exercise, and the weakness or disappearance by
the disuse, of an organ.   It is for physiologists

to explain this. In some cases they can do so.
The use of an organ draws more blood,
"wherein is the life," to it. However we may
account for it, it is a fact with which we are all
familiar, that the use of an organ makes it more
useful, and thus leads to the farther use of it.
The fisherman's chest expands, and the plough-
man's limbs become stronger, by the employ-
ment which they give them. Useless organs
disappear when they become cumbersome, as
the two first and the two last toes have done in
the foot of a horse.

(3) There are the small increments and dec-
rements of organisms produced by the action
of the elements and internal movements.
These may continue and become hereditary.
Thus a member may be cut off, or an augmen-
tation made to it. There may be at times an
extraordinary birth, which to a limited extent
modifies the model form. By such retarda-
tions and accelerations, as they have been
called, cumulative changes are produced, which
go down to future generations. This is an
agency much dwelt on by Cope and Hyatt,
and it is undoubtedly acting everywhere in
nature, and helping to produce the great number of variations in individuals, and, perhaps,

even in species which we observe clustering round the generic type.

These modifications are produced very much by the environment of the organism, which is always liable to be influenced by the company which it keeps. But as all organisms are complex, that is, have various elements, there may be changes produced by the interaction of internal forces, as, for example, when the plant or animal grows, or when it decays. It is certain that by these influences, and it may be by others, known or unknown, varieties are produced; some think even new species. Religion has nothing to say against this, and observation has much to say in its favor.

X.

HOMOLOGIES WITH ADAPTATIONS.—The two facts which show design are order and adaptation, general order and special adaptations. They are seen in human workmanship, where we have houses, machines, clocks, watches, formed on a plan, but the parts made to accomplish special ends. They are seen in Divine workmanship, where we have common forms, with adjustments to a purpose; what I have called Typical Forms and Special ends. The common causes produce the general order, being so collocated by Him who instituted them. As they act they produce changes which by the same Divine wisdom accomplish particular ends.

In all animate nature we have homologies— that is, common forms adapted to different purposes. Thus in plants we have the petals, stamens, and pistils of the flower, all after the leaf type, according to the discovery of Goethe. I have shown that the tree, its branches, and its branchlets, are after the same form—that is of a leaf, as determined by its ribs. The four typical limbs of vertebrate animals become fins in fishes, wings in birds, feet in mammals, and two of them hands in man. There are typical vertebræ running along the backbone, but differing in different parts of the column, and with special appendages, in wings, and arms, and other useful organs.

There are also homologies in invertebrate animals not so determinate and often difficult to detect, but very instructive in showing a plan in the formation of these lower creatures, and some of them pointing on to the vertebrate structure, and to man himself : as when the limbs of a lobster are variously developed and used as jaws, walking and running organs, as well as for moving the gills, and supplying them

with a stream of water. It has been found that
all the vertebrates and all the invertebrates, except the Protozoa, agree together in their early
development from an egg by germ-layers, from
which the different organs of the adult animals
are variously produced.

Of the two factors the former—that is, the
general order—is the more prominent in the
types of the older naturalists and of Cuvier,
and the other, that of specialty, is seen in the
modifications produced by the environment,
according to Lamarck, St. Hilaire, and Darwin. The two are illustrated by the arrangement of plants by Linnæus, one of the great
classifiers of nature, under a binomial division
of genera and species, the former representing
the common resemblance, and the latter the
special difference.

Now, the doctrine of development gives us a
glimpse of the way in which the organs have
been formed and varied to accomplish an end
necessary to the existence of the plant and animal. It shows us, too, how organs disappear at
times, leaving only a rudimental form, as evidence, like tombstones, of their once having
lived. They have shrunk because no longer
used, being no longer of use. Thus we have

the mammæ, in male animals, the sightless eyes
of fishes in the Adalberg and Kentucky caves,
and the rudimentary teeth in the young of
whales.

I venture to suggest that seeds are the ho-
mologues of the whole plant, and the germ of
the whole animal, being concentrations of these
ingredients, and the product varying according
to the ingredients present. Von Baer has shown
that there is a most remarkable parallelism between the embryology of the individual, and the
past history of the race. Animals start in the
womb as a single cell, and though there is no
doubt a difference, the embryo of man cannot
be distinguished from that of a worm. But as
the human embryo grows it becomes like a fish,
a reptile, a mammal, and finally takes the human form. It thus passes through the series
of the ramified classification of animals given
above, the kingdom, sub-kingdom, class, order,
family, genus, and species. " On the hypothesis of evolution this parallelism has a meaning;
indicates the primordial kinship of all organisms and that progressive differentiation of them
which the hypothesis alleges. But on any other
theory the parallelism is meaningless." [1]

---

[1] Conn's " Evolution of To-Day," p. 144.

XI.

ARE SPECIES UNCHANGEABLE?—It is acknowledged on all hands, by evolutionists as well as
anti-evolutionists, that all plants and animals
belong to a natural species. This distinction
has a safe place in the economy of nature. It
accomplishes most important ends. It keeps
nature from running into inextricable confusion. It makes organic nature comprehensible
and usable by human intelligence.

So deep is the distinction, that about two
centuries ago naturalists laid it down as a
maxim, that species are so fixed as to be im-
mutable—as the law of gravitation is. There
are people who ask us, with a look of absolute
incredulity and scorn : Do you really believe
and have the effrontery to maintain that by
natural law the lily can be changed into a rose
and a sheep into a goat ? The fixity of species
has become (it was not so in ancient times) a
religious doctrine, and a sacred feeling has
gathered around it which it is dangerous to
disturb. It is certain that species are so fixed
that they cannot readily be changed. It is
certain that God has so arranged natural law
that combinations have been formed that cannot be dissevered by any ordinary law. No
one believes that by natural selection a deer

can be turned into a horse, or a cow into an elephant. It is allowed that species are not so fixed as to prevent varieties. These often differ very widely from the original stock and from one another. What a difference exists in the pigeons, in their forms and colors, while they have all sprung from the rock pigeon. What a diversity in the roses, which have all come from the common dog rose. The breeds of dogs vary in size, in shape, in gentleness or fierceness, but are believed to be descended from some wolf-like creature. There are said to be about twelve species of horse, all descended from the Eohippus, and he from an older ungulate who lived a hundred of millions of years ago.

It is often urged as an objection to the theory of evolution, that the varieties and breeds of domestic animals which have been produced by the agency of man, are apt when allowed to run wild to return to the original type. It is not difficult to explain the actual facts in accordance with evolution as it is explained in this treatise. In the progress of development animals assume a fixed structure which they naturally retain and cannot easily be changed. But when placed in new surroundings alterations may be produced. These will continue as long as the environment continues the same ; that is, as long as the animal is in a state of domestication.   But when it is placed back in its old position, its old nature still remaining in it will bring it back to its old form.   Darwin mentions the case of domestic rabbits which were carried to the Isle of Porto Santo, near Madeira, in 1618 or 1619, A.D., and became there very different from any domestic breed, as well as from the original species.   They are much smaller than the European rabbits. " The upper fur is redder, with few or no black hairs ; the throat and belly are generally pale gray or leaden color instead of pure white." " The males of the Porto Santo rabbits refuse to associate or breed with the domestic varieties." When these rabbits were brought back to the London Zoölogical Garden, they began to assume the appearance of the English wild rabbit ; the edging of the ears and upper surface of the tail became blackish-gray, and the whole body much less red.   " Thus, on returning them to their original European environment, the characters of the parent wild species, which had been dormant at Porto Santo, began to reassert themselves." [1]

---

[1] Darwin : " The Variation of Plants and Animals under Domestication," vol. i., pp. 141–144.

The whole tendency of nature is to prevent the mixture of species, which in most departments is impossible, which in some cases is unnatural and restrained by the sterility of the offspring, and can never occur except in rare and exceptional cases. All the while it is not so easy to determine wherein a species differs from its congeners, and as to certain breeds, whether they are varieties or different species. A species is not constituted by mere external agreement, for creatures very like each other may belong to very different species and genera. The only decisive point which can now be fixed on as separating species is the infertility of the offspring produced by crossing. The offspring of different species when they pair are supposed to be unfertile. But it is urged by our advanced naturalists that even this mark is failing the anti-evolutionists. It is affirmed that there are hybrids which breed and continue to breed. It is known that there are different domestic races which cross and yet continue fertile. It is alleged that natural races may do the same, and that in rare cases the fertility of hybrids seems slightly greater than that of the legitimate young.[1] It does

---

[1] Conn's "Evolution of To-Day," chap. I.

not appear that the crossing of different
species of plants leads to sterility. It is a
question for science to settle and not religion,
which does not seem to me to have any special
interest in the question, though it is gratified to
find that there are such limits to the crossing
of natural kinds as to prevent breeds from
running into confusion.

It has often been demanded of evolutionists
that they present before our eyes a case of one
species being changed into another. Evolutionists argue that this is unreasonable, as such
transformations can take place only by slow
processes, which cannot be noticed by any
observer. This answer has commonly been
regarded as sufficient. But now it is said that
an actual transformation has been observed.
A Russian naturalist, Schmankewitsch, had
noticed that a species of crustacea, Artemia
Milhausenii, has been changed by the gradual
freshening of a salt-water lake in which the
creature lived. Acting on the principle involved, he added salt to the water till he
changed the species into another (A. Salina),
which again he transformed into a third.
Freshening the water, it was turned into still
another creature which had been ranked as a

distinct genus by naturalists.[1]   Let this case
be thoroughly sifted by scientific men, who
will determine for us whether the new creatures
produced are mere varieties or really new
species and genera. I am sure meanwhile that
religion is safe whatever be the decision
come to.

I have never been able to see that religion,
and in particular that Scripture in which our
religion is embodied, is concerned with the
question of the absolute immutability of species.
Final Cause, which is a doctrine of natural religion, should be satisfied with species being
so fixed as to secure the stability of nature. If
new species appear in our world, they differ so
slightly from the old, out of which they have
been formed, that there are no violent or revo-
lutionary changes involved. Nature is kept
steadfast and theism is satisfied, even though
in rare circumstances a new species should be
produced to diversify nature and make it equal
to the duty of peopling the earth, which is certainly one of the purposes of God by which he
widens the sphere of happiness.

---

[1] Conn's " Evolution of To-day," p. 26.

CHAPTER II.

I.

THE FORMATIVE PERIOD OF THE EARTH.—
"No one can find out the work which God
doeth from the beginning unto the end."
Science does not know what was the beginning,
nor whether there has been a beginning in
God's doings ; nor does it know the end, for
there will be no end.   But we know that our
mundane system, especially our earth, has had
a beginning, and we can so far trace its history.
According to the well-known theory of Kant
and Laplace, started by each independently of
the other, there is a mass of matter with an
impulse given to it rotating from west to east,
and throwing off the earth as a fiery liquid, to
move in the same direction.   As the earth ro-
tates it is formed into an oblate spheroid.   As
it cools it has a solid crust with thick, gaseous
substances surrounding it, which, in the process
of time, are condensed into water.   As it then

presents itself, it is composed of seventy elements, less or more, and in it are mechanical, chemical, gravitating forces, probably also magnetic and electric—whatever these may be.[1] As they operate, divisions and combinations take place—what are called differentiations and concentrations. The atmosphere is separated from the land, and, as the oscillations of the crackling earth go on, portions of land rise above the waters. " Mountain chains," says Le Conte, " seem to be produced by the secular cooling, and, therefore, contraction of the earth, greater in the interior than the exterior, in consequence of which the face of the old earth is become wrinkled." As yet there is no sun ; which, in fact, is being condensed out of the nebular mass, but light and heat are generated, ready to nourish the tiny plants which are ready to spring up on the rocks lying under the waters. In all this God is working, not by special interferences, but by the natural causes which develop into effects—in other words, by evolution. So far, there is no difference of opinion. All is by evolution.

---

[1] There is a central truth in Laplace's theory, but, to account for the whole phenomena, a place must be given to the powers referred to above.

II.

THE ARCHAIC OR EOZOIC AGE.—In the long formative period there was no life; indeed, there could have been none, owing to the intense heat. Life appears first in the Laurentian rocks which stretch through Canada, where they are 40,000 feet in depth, on into the United States, and are also found in Scotland, and bulk largely in Bohemia. These are not primary rocks, for they are formed of matter carried by rivers into the sea. In them are found the Eozoon, of so amorphous a character that it has been disputed whether it is an animal or a mere mineral. If there were animals, there must also have been plants, vitalizing minerals, to feed them. We know otherwise that there must have been life, from the graphite and limestone in the formation. Life has appeared. How? Certainly from the God who made the world. Was it by God's immediate fiat, or by evolution? The question is started; the discussion of it may be adjourned till we have the facts fully before us. Meanwhile it is certain that from this date we have evolution—every plant and every animal from an ancestry.

III.

THE SILURIAN, THE AGE OF INVERTEBRATES, SPECIALLY OF MOLLUSCS.—The formation lies unconformably on the Laurentian, showing long deposits and numerous upheavals. It is found in the borders of Wales and in the State of New York, and in many other places. There is now an abundance of plants, mainly marine, chiefly algæ, or sea-weeds. Animals are also numerous, such as sponges, radiates, corals, forming reefs, medusæ, jelly-fishes. There are fossils of beautiful graptolites, of stemmed echinoderms and crinoids. There are cephalopods, the most highly organized and most powerful of the tribe ; they are represented in the present day by the nautilus, the squid, and cuttle-fishes. In this age articulated animals appear, specially soft fleshy worms, not preserved themselves, but two hundred species are made known by their tracks and borings, so important in producing soil. In the Lower Silurian there is no evidence of terrestrial or fresh-water life. In the Upper Silurian there are remains of terrestrial plants, such as club-mosses. I am pleased to observe that these are branched at definite angles, like the trees which come at a late date. In the trilobites, which now reach their maximum size, well constructed eyes are visible of the invertebrate type. It is said that before the Silurian age closes, may be found vertebrates of a low type.

IV.

THE DEVONIAN AGE, WHICH MAY BE CALLED
THE FISH AGE.—Hitherto the plants have been
chiefly marine.   Now land plants are abundant ; and we discover many that are still with
us, ferns, lycopods, equisetæ, also advanced
conifers, which may have covered some parts
of the earth with forests.   "In the Hamilton
beds the evidences of verdure over the land are
abundant.   The remains show that there were
trees, as well as smaller plants ; that there were
forests of moderate growth, and great jungles
over wide-spread marshes." [1]

There are peat-bogs and submerged forests,
anticipations of the coming Coal Measures.
Insects enliven the forests, and have organs to
issue sounds which probably imply ears to
hear them.   The fishes which first came are
ganoids, and sharks, some of them three
feet thick and from fifteen to eighteen feet
long.   The more elegant forms of teleosts,
which now swim in our seas have not yet appeared.   "The most fundamental law of evolution," says Le Conte, "where is differentiation," *i. e.*, a separating of generalized into several specialized forms, a separation of one

---

[1] Dana's " Geology," p. 268.

stem into several branches. The Devonian
fishes are an admirable illustration of this law.
The first introduced fishes were not typical
fishes, but sauroids—*i. e.*, fishes, which combined with their distinctive fish characters others
which allied them with reptiles. They were the
representatives and progenitors of both classes.
From this common stem diverge two branches,
viz., typical fishes on the one hand, and reptiles
on the other. "This is but one example of a
very general law which may be formulated
thus : The first introduced of any class or order were not typical representatives of that
class or order, but connecting links with other
classes or orders, the complete separation of
two or more classes or orders being the result
of subsequent evolution."[1]

V.

THE CARBONIFEROUS OR GREAT PLANT AND
COAL AGE.—The great classes and orders of
plants scatter, and are more firmly organized
than in any other age. Between 2,000 and
3,000 fossil plants have been found, and one
fourth of them are of this formation. The
lower forms of plant life continue, but rising
above them are the ramified forms of conifers,

---

[1] " Geology," p. 332.

lepidodendrons, sigillariæ, and calamites.
These sinking in a warm, moist, stifling climate, and in stagnant water, become hardened
by heat and pressure into coal. It is the
great coal-bearing era with its sandstones,
shales, and lime-stones, and with metalliferous
veins running through them. Without the
plant deposits, and the power from the sun
stored up in them, human factories and man's
working capacity would have been greatly limited. There are Coal Measures with a thick-
ness of 10,000 feet, indicating what a length
of time this age must have lasted. The fishes
become reptilian in character, and amphibia
make their appearance. The Palæozoic now
passes away, and a new era appears.

VI.

THE MESOZOIC AGE, THAT OF REPTILES.—
It is divided into the Triassic, Jurassic, and
Cretaceous. It is not necessary in this epitome
to give a separate account of each of these.
The plants are still making coal in the Jurassic
period. Vegetation consists mainly of such
plants as ferns, cycads, and conifers ; but higher
forms uppear. In this latter age the highest
forms of plants, dicotyledons, come forth.
Fossils of the trees with which we are familiar

are found, such as oaks, willows, poplars, sassi-
fras, dog-wood, maple, hickory, beach, walnut,
sweet gum, laurel, fig, sequoia, tulip.

In this age reptiles reign in the sea, on the
land, and in the air, some of them crawling, such
as saurians and crocodiles ; but some standing
and moving on their hind legs, thereby antici-
pating birds and man himself ; and some of
them, such as the pterodactyls, flying, and
warm-blooded like mammals.   In the Jurassic
the Atlantosaurus, discovered by Marsh, seems
to have been nearly 100 feet in length and 30
in height.   To show how the forms run into
each other, Dana says : " As in birds the bones
of pterodactyls are hollow, to fit them for flying ; but unlike birds they have the skin, claws,
and teeth of reptiles. Their habits were those of
bats rather than birds." [1]   Birds come forth
fully developed in this age ; some of them not
capable of flight.   Birds begin in long-tailed
or reptilian species; six species have been
found with teeth.   Some of the reptiles have
mammalian characters, especially in the teeth.
In the later deposits are found mammals nearly all of them marsupials and insectivorous.
The character of the age is summed up by

---

[1] Dana's " Geology," p. 446.

Dana : " It is the era of the first mammals, the first birds, the first of the common or osseous fishes, and the first palms and angiosperms." [1] The disturbance which in America closed the Mesozoic period, upheaved half the continent.

VII.

The Cenozoic Age, That of Mammals.— " The ages," says Geikie, " of lycopods, ferns, cycads, and yew-like conifers have passed away, and that of dicotyledons and angiosperms, of the hard-wood trees and evergreens, now succeeds ; but not by sudden extinction and re-creation, for, as we have seen, some of these trees had already begun to make their appearance even in Cretaceous times." [2] The early animals were chiefly herbivorous, such as the Phenacodus, Coryphodon, and Hyracotherium. The age of reptiles is past, and marsupials are very much confined to Australia. In the fossils, we discover the remains of such animals as eagles, owls, and woodpeckers ; nearly all the genera and many of the species of plants and also of invertebrates are the same as at present. This age closes with the great Glacial epoch, in which a great portion of the earth was covered with ice and snow,

---

[1] " Geology," p. 403   [2] " Geology," p. 837.

believed to have been 7,000 feet thick in Norway, and the temperature intensely cold. We see traces of it in the striated rocks, in our mountains, and in boulders often carried to long distances. The great ice sheets of Switzerland and Norway are remnants of it. The cold led to the destruction of many species of plants and animals, and the migrations of others toward warmer regions. In this age placentals, such as monkeys, make their appearance.

VIII.

THE QUATERNARY AGE, THAT OF THE LARGEST MAMMALS.—Plants and animals have become what they now are. Plants identical with species living all over Europe retreat to the northern regions and are found in high altitudes. In South America animals take the form of sloths, armadillos and llamas. In various countries mammals take a gigantic size, such as the extinct elks, the mammoth and mastodon. This mammal age gives way to that of man—intelligent and responsible man.

IX.

INFERENCES.—The above is a brief and necessarily imperfect geological history. We perceive that :

1. There is what scientists call system, what platonists call an idea, what theologians call design or purpose, in the history of organic life. It is produced by God, but the question arises, whether without, or with, creature instrumentality, and the further question, whether the instrumentality, if there be such, can be discovered by human research.

2. There is a gradual rise ; through millions of years, or rather ages, of vegetable and animal life. The question is, whether this can be produced by evolution, always under God. It will be generally admitted that the formation of the mere matter of the earth, its seas, mountains, and rivers, have been effected by natural causes. May it not be the same with the growth of the organic world, it being always understood that the causes are different ?

3. It is admitted that the individual plant and animal are generated from a parent. May it not be the same with the vegetable races— the horse we ride on, from an older and diminutive horse, birds and marsupials from certain forms of reptiles ? There is nothing atheistic in this supposition.

4. We have convincing evidence of the descent of races from older races. I have already

given the details as to the horse. We have
many other cases, these increasing as new
regions are explored. The very Eohippos
seems to have been a descent from the ungu-
lates.

"In the earliest Tertiary deposits of North
America," says Prof. Scott to me, "we
find a series of five-toed plantigrade animals from which all the hoofed animals
have descended, the difference between the
various groups having been continually aug-
mented with the process of time. The genealogy of the tapir and rhinoceros has now been
completely made out, running back to a common ancestor in the early Tertiary formations.
Step by step changes in the character of the
dentition, and of all parts of the skeleton have
been accumulated, until they result in animals of
a very different character. In the same manner
the passage from pig-like animals to the rumi-
nants has been demonstrated, and the recent
discovery of a five-toed ruminant proves the
origin of the ruminating animals from the
primitive common ancestors of all hoofed animals including even the elephant.

" The history of the Camel and Llama tribes
is well understood ; beginning with very small

four-toed animals with complete series of teeth
in both jaws; then passing to forms in which
only the two median, the third and fourth, of
the original series are preserved; then these
two fuse into a single cannon bone, some
of the teeth are lost, and the limbs lengthen,
the animals become larger, till the modern
form is reached. Rütimayer has proved
the gradual derivation of the Ox tribe from
antelope-like animals, these from deer-like
forms, and these again from the primitive
pig-like types. In the case of the carnivora,
we have clear evidence of their descent from
insectivorous animals; and it has lately been
proved that all of the land carnivora have been
derived from the primitive dog-like animals of
the Eocene territory. Transitional types between these animals and the bear series on the
one hand, and the cat and hyena series on the
other, are now abundantly known. There are
many groups, it need hardly be said, as to
which our information is still very incomplete,
but new discoveries are continually announced
which widen the horizon for us. It seems
hardly too much to say that before many years
the genealogy and inter-relationships of all
mammalian groups will be fairly understood."

5. We have numerous examples of transition cases. Professor Scott says : "The earliest known birds, Archæopteryx, from the Jurassic formation, are amazingly close to reptiles in structure. They possess teeth of reptilian types, without a beak, in the modern sense of the word ; the structure of the hand was unlike that of any living bird, in that the fingers were all free (*i. c.*, not fused into one mass), and all had claws ; the foot can hardly be distinguished from that of some reptiles; the tail was like that of a lizard, but with a pair of feathers attached to each joint. It is particularly worthy of note that these peculiarities, even the possession of teeth, are reproduced in the embryos of modern birds. On the other hand, certain of the extinct reptiles approach these birds very closely in all points of structure, so that almost the only mark of separation between the two groups, birds and reptiles, is the presence or absence of feathers. Thus palæontology and embryology agree perfectly in the derivation of birds from reptiles." "The two pairs of fins in fishes represent the two pairs of limbs of higher species ; an air-bladder, the lungs ; a loose-bone in a closed cavity, the ear."[1]

---

[1] Dana's " Geology," p. 594.

It is well known that aquatic animals have
become suited to a terrestrial life.   The air
bladder of certain fishes, such as the mud
fishes of Africa, came to possess a respiratory
function, and developed as a lung.   In the tad-
pole we see the gill, but it is superseded by the
lung.   The male animal has mammæ ; the un-
born whale has rudimentary teeth ; in the pi-
thon there are rudiments of limbs.   The whales
and porpoises are like fish, but science declares
them to be mammals.

We discover cases in which the distinctions
supposed to be deepest in the organic kingdoms are effaced.   The main distinction in
plants is between the monocotyledons, which
have parallel veins, and the dicotyledons, which
have curved veins ; yet we have the arum and
smilax, which are monocotyledons, and yet
have reticulated leaves.   Often have I seen
the sun-dew plant sucking in insects and feeding on them, which shows that the difference
between plant and animal is capable of being
bridged over.[1]   But perhaps the most striking

---

[1] Often on the Grampians of Scotland have I watched the beautiful
sun-dew plant drawing in insects and dissolving them.   Had I published this when I first noticed it, I might have anticipated Darwin
in his discovery of flesh-eating plants.   I failed to do this and lost
my chance of becoming famous ! ! !

case is that in which there are exceptions to
the law, which was supposed to be fixed and
unchangeable, that all mammals bring forth
their young alive—that is, are viviparous.
These curious animals, the Duck-bill and the
spiny Ant-eater, are truly mammals, yet the
eggs laid by them have been found within the
last few years in Australia by Caldwell and
Haacke, showing that they are oviparous. All
this does not prove that there is no such thing
as Natural Kinds, or that there are no fixed
distinctions in nature, and that therefore nature is not settled ; it shows merely that there
are variations which diversify the unity in our
world, and have this further advantage, that
they show us the way in which nature works
to produce an infinite diversity in the midst of
sameness.

6. A confirmation of the theory of the evolution of races is found in the circumstance
that in islands far removed from continents, as,
for instance, Bermuda, St. Helena, the Gala-
pagos, and through the Malayan Archipelago,
there are no mammals. Quadrupeds have
been produced on continents, and are not capable of swimming into these separated places.
In these same islands are no species of frogs,

toads, or newts, as their spawns are killed by salt water. There are no placental mammals in Australia, except perhaps rats, which was separated from Asia before placental mammals had been gendered. If new species are necessarily the immediate creation of God, one does not see how he should not have created these in islands as well as on continents.

The following summary has been drawn out by Prof. Cope : " The mammalia have been traced to the theromorphous reptiles through the monotremata. The birds, some of them, at least, appear to have been derived from the dinosaurian reptiles. The reptiles in the primary representative order, the theromorpha, have been probably derived from the rhachitomous batrachia. The batrachia have originated from the sub-class of fishes, the dipnoi, though not from any known form. I have shown that the true fishes, or teleostomi, have descended from an order of sharks, the ichthyotomi, which possess characters of the dipnoi also. The origin of the sharks remains entirely obscure, as does also that of the pisces as a whole. Dohrn believes the marsipobranchii to have acquired their present characters by a process of degeneration. The origin of the

vertebrata is as yet entirely unknown, Kowal-
evsky deriving them from the ascidians and
Semper from the annelida." [1]

All this does not mathematically demonstrate
that evolution is and must be universal.   It is
conceivable that in regions yet unexplored
there may be cases in which vegetable and animal life may have been produced otherwise
than by parentage.   But it is equally true that
we cannot prove that gravitation must be
necessarily universal.   There may be worlds
or, it is supposable, spots in our world, where
bodies are held together by a different law
from that discovered by Newton.   All that can
be done by mere observation in either case
is to show that there is such a law ex-
tensively prevailing, with no known exception.   But at this point there comes in the
more universal law, established by a wide and
uncontradicted experience, that nature is uniform.   We are entitled to argue that the law
of gravitation, being so wide-spread, is a law of
nature, and must be operating in places of the
earth or planets of which we know nothing.
On the same ground evolutionists infer that
the development of living beings is so general

---

[1] Cope's "Origin of the Fittest," p. 317.

that it must be universal throughout the organic world. But while the law of genetic descent is universal, it does not therefore follow that there is no other power involved in the genesis of our earth and the direction of its history. Every one acknowledges that gravitation has universal sway in our mundane system, but there are powers of chemical affinity, of capillary attraction, of electric and magnetic motion, also operating, which act with, or stay, or control the law of gravity : thus, magnetism will hold up a piece of metal which would otherwise fall to the ground. At this point extreme evolutionists are to be met, by showing that there are other powers which have acted with it or have limited it. I am to show that while there are universal laws of descent there are other powers necessary to the origination and continuance of the world.

CHAPTER III.

I.

OTHER AGENTS BESIDES EVOLUTION.—There are agents performing an essential part in the formation and continuation of our world which are not mentioned, except incidentally, by geologists. There are some things which cannot be brought into the physicist's laboratory, and which therefore he may not be required specially to discuss; but he should not in his narrowness disparage or ridicule those who insist on looking at them and finding out the part which they play. I will do no more than refer to the creation of matter, to show that it has not been overlooked. But it is of importance to bring into view and meditate on certain agents which have played a most important part in the formation of our world, but which cannot, so far as we see, be evolved from the material which we have been considering.

47

II.

LIGHT.—We do not know all the mystery of its action. It consists of vibrations in an ether. When and whence came that ether with its properties? There is no evidence that it has developed in the ordinary action of matter. It is certain that it performs a very important part in the economy of nature. It is necessary to the growth of plants and animals. Perhaps no one can tell whether it has come from an antecedent mundane matter, or whether, like matter itself and its forces, mechanical, chemical, gravitating, it may not be the immediate product of the creative power of God, who said, " Let there be light, and there was light."

III.

LIFE.—Geology shows an indefinitely long azoic period in the history of our world. Life appears first when plants appear. It is not, like extension and mechanical power, of the essence of matter. The great mass of matter has no life. No chemical, magnetic, or electric force can produce it. No scientific man can manufacture it in his laboratory. It is something superinduced upon ordinary matter upon the four elements, oxygen, hydrogen, nitrogen, and carbon, which it turns to its uses. It pos-

sesses very marked properties : it has a power
of Assimilation, such as the Crystal, the highest form of dead matter, does not possess, it
draws in the elements, and transforms them
into its own living body ; it has a power of
Growth, and may expand a germ into the swell-
ing tree or the huge mastodon ; it has a power
of Reproduction, gendering a seed which genders other life ; it is intended that there should
be a series of creatures enjoying life, and so it
has a power of Waste whereby it dies, but
leaves behind it a new life.

IV.

SENSATION.—This appears in the animal in
the Eozoic, or at least in the Palæozoic ages.
It is allowed that ordinary matter does not possess feeling.   There is no proof that vegetable
life has it, though in our poetical moments we
fondly believe that there are leaves and flowers
with a sensitive nature.   We are now in a
higher region than the corporeal ; we are beyond the physical ; we are in the psychical.

This sensation cannot be defined so as to
make it comprehensible to any who have not
felt it.   It is known, its very nature is, to all
who have experienced it, so that explanation is
not needed by them, and no explanation can

make it clearer to them. The creatures that
have sensation have also a power of locomo-
tion. Henceforth much of the activity of the
world arises from animals seeking pleasure and
avoiding pain. I defy any one to show that
this sensation so varied, often so strong, can
be produced from any of the powers previously
existing on the earth, nor even from Life—in
the plants we have life, but no feeling.

V.

INSTINCT.—There may be animals which
have sensation, but with no instinct. But instinct appears very early in the animal kingdom. We have now more than life, more than
feeling—there is a low kind of thought. It
takes most remarkable forms in insects, such as
ants and bees, which perform deeds of which
they cannot be supposed to know the full
meaning. Animals lay up food in summer to
provide nourishment for them in the winter, of
which they cannot have any clear conception.
The mother duck makes it appear as if she
could not fly, to allure the dog to follow
her, and thus allow the ducklings to escape.
The curlew places its bare nest on a place from
which there runs a hollow, and down this it
runs when a boy approaches, and raises a cry

at some distance to allure the boy from her eggs or young. Instinct rises higher in more advanced animals, such as horses, elephants, and dogs. It is natural and original, and does not depend on experience, though to a small extent it can take advantage of experience. We have now anticipation of intelligence. There is now memory ; animals remember the blow, and the person inflicting it. There is imagination ; dogs, as Aristole says, hunt in their dreams. There seem to be low kinds of reasoning, or at least of the association of ideas, on which reasoning so much depends.

VI.

INTELLIGENCE.—This may not be altogether independent of instinct, of whose acts it sees the meaning and makes use of them ; but it is something higher. It looks at the nature of things, at their forms, colors, properties; and can discover the causes of things. " We know in part." It can abstract, generalize, and reason, and rise to an imperfect idea of the infinite. It can look far back into the past, and far forward into the future. It can devise means to accomplish ends. It can entertain feelings of sympathy and kindness, and it grieves over the decease of companions.

VII.

MORALITY and the higher intelligence are closely connected, and may have come in together. By the latter, we discover what things are; by the former, what they ought to be. Morality, then, reveals something higher. It shows us the distinction between good and evil, and lays man under obligation to attend to the one and avoid the other. We have now reached the highest eminence which this world has yet attained: the age of moral and responsible man.

VIII.

HOW HAVE THESE AGENTS COME IN? BY WHAT CAUSE?—I maintain that no one of them could have been produced by the ordinary powers of nature.

It is a law of causation anticipated, as can be shown, from an old date that a cause—I am speaking only of physical causes—can give only what it possesses. Causation cannot create any thing new; it cannot give what it has not within itself. There is nothing in the effect which was not potentially in the cause; that is, in the agents which constitute the cause. There is no proof that any of the agents just named, say sensation, or intelligence, were in the atoms, or in the mechanical or chemical powers. But there is a point of time at which they appear, when the first pain or pleasure is felt, and the first perception of things takes place. The powers once introduced continue ever afterwards to act. Their appearance, from whatever cause they spring, constitutes an epoch. Their action is not inconsistent with the great geological changes, but is coincident with them, and operates in producing them.

Whence came they? How come they—the vibrating ether constituting light? So far as life is concerned, it is still true—*omne vivum ab ovo.* Our highest scientific men, even those most prepossessed in favor of the doctrine, allow that there has been no case produced of spontaneous generation—that is, of life proceeding from any thing but antecedent life. Whence, then, the first life? If there be a difficulty in getting life by evolution from the lifeless, there is much more in getting some of the other agents, say sensation from mechanical force, or instinct from chemical combination, or intelligence from electricity, or morality from all combined—say the morality of Joseph, " How can I do this great wickedness

and sin against God?" When these agents
are generated they develop like products;
from life proceeds life, and intelligence gener-
ates intelligence. But no mundane power can
produce them at first, and it is reasonable that
we should refer their production to God, to
whom all power belongs, even the power of
evolution. As evolution by physical causes
cannot do it, we infer that God does it by an
immediate fiat, even as he created matter and
the forces which act in matter. We certainly
know no other power capable of doing it. This
seems a legitimate conclusion. It calls in a
power known otherwise to work, and to be
competent to produce the effect. It makes
God continue the work of creation, and if
God's creation be a good work, why should he
not continue it?—often it may be with seasons
of cessation that the already created agents
may fully develop themselves. He may be a
continuous creator as he is a continuous pre-
server, thus widening and enlarging the sphere
of his wisdom and of his love.

IX.

HAVE THEY COME BY CREATURE AGENCY?—
There may be, indeed, another supposition.
Instead of creating immediately these powers,

God may have evolved them out of other
agencies. But if so, it is clear that these have
been called in at an appropriate time to produce the life, and the feeling, and the moral
discernment. In this case the change necessary to be made in our statement would be, to
make the appearance of these high agencies an
act of Providence instead of an act of Creation. It may be allowable to put the supposition for a moment that these agents have
been produced by some creature, when it will
be discovered that there is no advantage in it,
for the supposed producing powers are unknown to us, and evidently must forever remain unknown. We believe that there must
have been an act of creation out of nothing at
the beginning ; and the probable conclusion is
that epochal creations have been continued,
not interfering with the previous work, but in
the way of multiplying and expanding it indefinitely.

X.

THE NEW POWERS ARE SUPERINDUCED UPON
THE OLD.—It should be observed of these
powers, when they come they do not imply or
require the extinction or disappearance of the
previously existing powers—as stronger ani-

mals often lead to the suppression of weaker.
On the contrary, the new capacities are thoroughly adapted to the old, act upon them and
with them, strengthen them and widen their
influence. Light is necessary to the health
both of plants and animals. Life gives new
powers to the mineral, makes it move and assume new positions, and take new and varied
forms of utility and beauty in the form of trees
and flowers, of insects and fishes, of birds and
quadrupeds, of man and woman. Sensation in
eating and drinking, in gregarious intercourse,
and the pairing of sexes, is the grand motive
to the activity of the animal creation in earth,
and sea, and sky. Instinct is the peculiar pre-
server and propagator of living beings all over
the globe. Intelligence makes man, always
because God has so appointed, the ruler of this
last era, and gives him " dominion over the
fish of the sea, over the fowl of the air, and
over the cattle and every creeping thing that
creepeth on the earth." Morality binds intelligent men to God above and to men and
animals below, by stronger bonds than evolution can by a common descent and a like nature.

XI.

THE OLD POWERS CONTINUE TO ACT WITH
THE NEW.—The new act upon the old, while

the old act upon the new, and the action is always a joint action, with an abiding conservation and a constant advance. The new and the higher take the old and the lower into themselves. The plant is formed out of the mineral, which is made to take the nobler forms of bird and beast. The animal cannot turn the mineral into food; in order to do this it needs to feed on the vegetable. Intelligence turns all these agents into use, to accomplish beneficent purposes. Morality would direct them all to holy ends.

CHAPTER IV.

I.

GOD IN EVOLUTION.—There is, or was, a wide-spread idea that the doctrine of development is adverse to religion. This has arisen mainly from the circumstance that it seems to remove God altogether, or at least to a greater distance from his works, and this has been increased by the circumstance that the theory has been turned to atheistic purposes. This impression is to be removed, first, by declaring emphatically that we are to look on evolution simply as the method by which God works. It is a forgotten circumstance that when Newton proclaimed the law of gravitation it was urged that he thereby took from God an important part of his works to hand it over to material mechanism, and the objection had to be removed in a quarto volume written by the celebrated mathematician, Maclaurin ; and this was the more easily done from the circumstance

58

that Newton was a man of profound religious convictions. The time has now come when people must judge of a supposed scientific theory, not from the faith or unbelief of the discoverer, but from the evidence in its behalf. They will find that whatever is true, is also good, and will in the end be favorable to religion.

A second erroneous impression needs to be effaced. Because God executes his purposes by agents, which it should be observed he has himself appointed, we are not therefore to argue that he does not continue to act, that he does not now act. He may have set agoing the evolution millions of years ago, but he did not then cease from his operation, and sit aloof and apart to see the machine moving. He is still in his works, which not only were created by him, but have no power without his indwelling. Though an event may have been ordained from all eternity, God is as much concerned in it as if he only ordained it now. God acts in his works now quite as much as he did in their original creation. The effects follow, the product is evolved, because he wills it, just as plants generate only when there is light shining on them; just as day continues only because the sun shines. A birth or a death may be brought about by a caused evolution, but the mother may rest assured that God is in both, rejoicing with her, or pitying her.

I hold that time is a reality, so perceived by our minds and so perceived by the Divine Mind. The *eternal now* spoken of by some of the schoolmen and by the poet Cowley is a contradiction. But while time, past, present, and future, is a reality to Deity, it may stand in a very different relation to him from what it is to us. Time, past and future, may be contemplated as immediately by him as time present is by us, and his love be literally an everlasting love, comprehending all time, as his omniscience does all space.

II.

FINAL CAUSE.—I do not propose in these lectures to prove anew the existence of God. This has been done so satisfactorily by a succession of able men since the days of Socrates that it does not need to be repeated. My aim rather is to show that the doctrine of evolution does not undermine the argument from Final Cause, but rather strengthens it by furnishing new illustrations of the wisdom and goodness

of God.[1] The proof from design proceeds on
the observation of things as adapted one to
another to accomplish a good end, and is
equally valid whether we suppose adjustment
to have been made at once or produced by a
process which has been going on for millions
of years.   There is proof of a designing mind
in the eye as it is now presented to us, with its
coats and humors, rods and cones, retina and
nerves, all co-operating with each other and
with the beams that fall upon them from suns
millions of miles away.   But there is further
proof in the agents having been brought into
relation by long processes all tending to the
one end. I value a gift received from the hand
of a father ; but I appreciate it more when I
learn that the father has been using many and
varied means to earn it for me.

III.

Is the Method of Evolution a Good One?
—I am not prepared to prove that evolution
is the best way in which God could have proceeded, or that there are no other ways equally
good in which he acts in other worlds.   All
that I profess to do is to show that the method

---

[1] We have two excellent works published in our day on this subject,
Saisset's "Final Cause," and Flint's " Theism."

is not unworthy of God ; that it is suited to man's nature ; that it accomplishes some good ends. It is to this extent that I would "justify the ways of God to man."

After all, however, as we do not see the end, as we only see half-done work, we cannot perceive the full wisdom of this mode of procedure. The common soldier did not discover all the wisdom of the military plans of Alexander the Great, of Julius Cæsar, of Napoleon, or of Grant, but he saw enough to convince him that they were skilful generals. This is our position in regard to God's works : we discover enough of the arc to calculate the rest ; and as we see so much wisdom in the little that we know, we argue that there is vastly more in the much that is beyond.

People will not readily be reconciled to evolution till they are convinced that it is promoting a beneficent end. We may advance some circumstances fitted to produce this conviction.

IV.

EVOLUTION PRODUCES A SUCCESSIVE ORDER IN THE ORGANIC WORLD.—The present is evolved from the past, and is developed into the future. There is thus one orderly constitution of things from the beginning unto the

end, making us feel how stable all things are
as one generation succeeds another. We inquire into the past in the assurance that, to
whatever point we go, we find the same laws
operating as now. The present is the offspring
of the past, and we can trace its progenitors
so far back. It is the seed of the future, and
we can anticipate what is to come, influence it
for good, and hand down our works to future
generations. We all feel the blessing of chil-
dren having parents and of parents having chil-
dren. Since the days of Newton, every one
sees how gravitation binds in one all contemporaneous nature, sun to planet and planet to
sun. We may now see how development binds
in one compact nature the whole of successive
nature, the past ages with the present and the
present with the future.

V.

DEVELOPMENT BY SMALL INCREMENTS SE-
CURES THE CONTINUITY OF NATURE.—The
continuity of things was fondly dwelt on by
Leibnitz and the theists of the last century,
who showed that objects formed connected
series, in which all the parts shaded gracefully
into each other; and that there is a gradation
from the lowest up to the highest, from the

sea-weeds to the tree, from the monad up to
the elephant, from the lowest intelligence up
to angel and archangel, and to God himself.
In this century science is seeking to determine
in what this continuity consists, and what are
the limits to it. When properly announced it
is seen to be a beneficent arrangement, securing the world from violent convulsions, from
breaks and separations. It is caused, always
by a divine arrangement, by means of the development of one thing from another, with
which it is thereby connected. There is thus a
permanence in the agents' working, with a pre-
scribed and restricted variety in their action.
There is a constancy in nature, but it is a constant change with a constant abiding.

VI.

It Secures Order and Adaptation in Nature.—These are the two principles in nature
which prove design ; each separately proves
the existence of intelligence ; when the two
are united, the evidence is more than doubled.
Development under God secures that the two
are combined, while each has its own place.
The common seed or stalk produces family
likenesses throughout nature, while the diver-
gences provide that each has its individuality,

by which it may be recognized. Thus in trees there is a trunk to give stability to the frame; this strikes off into branches which give a form to the whole; each branch is formed after the model of the tree, and gives off branchlets which are of a like shape; and the whole is clothed with leaves which are made, by the length and angles of their mid-ribs, to take the same form as the tree and its branches. In the higher animals, there is a backbone which gives a unity to the entire skeleton, and to it are attached as appendages various members of the body, each serving its purpose, such as ribs, feet, toes.

Lamarck at times used language which reads as if he said that the wishes of an animal may produce an organ; as if the wish of the animal to swim produced fins, and the wish to fly produced wings. I am not sure that the French naturalist meant this. If he did, he was evidently misinterpreting nature. There is will in the production, but it is the will of Him who arranged all things, and who has so arranged them that organs grow as they are used. Petals open to the sun and profit by the light, and roots grow toward their nourishment. We see fishermen with broad shoulders and strong arms, and ploughmen with stout limbs. We can conceive of no method of action by which combined plan and purpose can be so effectually secured as by evolution.

VII.

DEVELOPMENT SECURES PROGRESSION.—This is not necessary. There are numerous cases in nature of degeneration and the disappearance of races, because of their not being suited to their environment, when it is meant that they should cease to exist. But as these give way others take their place, according to the beneficial law of the survival of the fittest, and the weak races are driven out by the strong. Nature may tend first to differentiate and scatter; but then it integrates, mainly by evolution, which gathers up the parts and produces higher organisms.

Farmers have always believed in heredity, and take advantage of it to produce fine breeds of sheep and cattle, dogs and horses : of sheep bearing rich wool, or yielding good mutton ; of cows giving a flow of milk or supplying well-fed beef ; of dogs to hunt sheep or hunt game ; of horses to run swiftly, or drag loaded wagons. By a higher arrangement of nature, or rather, the God of nature, the organic world is progressing : the earth is covered with a richer vegetation, and there are cereals where before were only heaths and mosses, and man himself is farther removed from the savage state. We have thus a promise that our earth may become a perfect abode for a perfected man.

VIII.

THE METHOD OF DEVELOPMENT IS SUITED TO MAN'S FACULTIES.—Man is so constituted that he has to gather knowledge by experience. But of what use would experience be, if the future did not resemble the past? It has been shown, again and again, that God's procedure by uniform law is the only one which enables man, with his present nature, to lay plans in the ordinary business of life likely to be successful. Were there no such regularity he could not be sure that the sun will rise to-morrow, that seed-time will be followed by harvest, or that food will nourish him. But the successive uniformity and consistency of nature are determined by the law of evolution, whereby the present comes out of the past and goes down into the future, with both of which it has connections. Without this, our faculties being as they are, man's wisest counsels would have no certainty; not so much as a probability of success, and he would cease to devise and act, and in the end, cease to live. The method is suited to man,

and man to the method ; and this by the fore-
ordained purpose of God, who has made both
and adapted them to each other.

IX.

DIFFICULTIES OF THEISM.—Every one acknowledges that in looking on nature as the
work of God we meet with perplexities. Ques-
tions may be started which we cannot answer.
How are certain evils, disease and death, and
inevitable sorrow consistent with the justice
and love of God? I fully admit that there are
results following from the laws of God, which
it is not easy to reconcile with the omniscience
and benevolence of Deity.

Sir William Hamilton has made the remark
that no difficulty emerges in theology, which
has not appeared previously in philosophy. A
similar remark may be made as to evolution.
No difficulty arises on the theory of development, which does not meet us on the theory of
the immediate creation of every new individual
and species. The works of nature are equally
the works of God on the one supposition as on
the other, and the mysteries bear against God
in the one case as in the other. The difficulties
are swallowed up by the overwhelming evidence
which we have in behalf of the omniscience
and benevolence of God.

CHAPTER V.

I.

FARTHER EVIDENCE OF PURPOSE.—It is very generally admitted by evolutionists, by none more fully than Professor Huxley, that the theory of Evolution does not undermine or interfere in any way with the ordinary doctrine of Final Cause. The adaptation of one object or agent to another and their coöperation to accomplish a good end, to give a life and plan to the plant and comfort to the animal, are fondly believed by the great body of mankind to be a proof of design and of a designing mind. The force of the argument is not lessened by the circumstance that the skilful structures have been inherited. If man could produce a machine which not only does its work, say a watch to keep time, but genders another machine of a like kind with itself, every one would be impressed with the ingenuity of the structure. So the very circumstance that a plant and animal can reproduce another plant and animal is an evidence of a more far-sighted design. Evolution does not lessen the force of the teleological argument. The question is started, May not the union and conspiracy of forces involved in Evolution furnish new proof, as it certainly supplies new illustrations, of purpose and ends ?

As there are still so many unfilled-up gaps in the evolutionary process, I would speak on the subject cautiously and with reserve. At the present stage of investigation I would not employ an argument from Evolution as furnishing the primary proof of the existence of God. But surely those of us who believe in God on other grounds may trace in the development of Nature evidence of his wisdom and goodness. We see proofs of purpose and skill in Nature as it now presents itself to us, and we can connect this with the mode of production of the objects ; and we find the two, the present condition and past history, shedding light on each other. It is pleasant to think that when a new series of facts has been discovered reaching over thousands of ages, they teach the same lessons as the old facts which pressed themselves on the attention of our forefathers.

We see that contemporaneous · Nature fits in beautifully to successive Nature as it is unfolded in the ages. Evolution, like geology, was at first looked upon with suspicion by religious people. But geology has come to be a strengthener of faith as it displays new instances of design, and is confirmatory of Scripture as showing that creation has proceeded by epochs like the days of Genesis. We may now see that there is a wonderful plan not only in the present state of the vegetable and animal worlds, but in the method of their production by evolutionary causation. God acts everywhere in nature through means, and we may discover a fitness in the means. Evolution is thus in thorough harmony with all the other operations of Nature, showing the evidently designed adaptation of one thing to another in the past and in the present.

We see evidently in Nature certain subordinate ends planned and executed, always under the highest end, the manifestation of the wisdom and goodness of God to the contemplation of the intelligent creation. One of these is the preservation and advancement of species.

God, as it were, says to the plants and animals, " Be fruitful and multiply and replenish

the earth." The science of Evolution has
shown that these ends are accomplished in the
most effective manner by Natural Selection and
the other evolutionary instruments, such as the
surroundings of the living creature, the use
and disuse of organs, and, in the case of animals, the exercise of intelligence. These all
tend to the spread of order and ends. In particular, Natural Selection, with its consequent,
"the survival of the fittest," is a most beneficent provision. All the new organs have a
use, are produced because they have a use ;
they continue as long as they are useful, and
they commonly disappear when they have no
longer a purpose to serve. Evolutionists are
speaking and writing constantly of the use and
usefulness of organs. Even those who have
no belief in an intelligent use are obliged to
employ the language to express the fact, and
this because the fact exists. I could quote mul-
titudes of passages to this effect from our most
determined evolutionists, including Darwin
and Spencer. Dr. Wallace sums up : " The
shape, the size, and the colors of the petals,
even the specks and spots with which they are
adorned, the position in which they stand, the
movements of the stamens and pistils at vari-

ous times, especially at the period of and just
after fertilization, have been proved to be
strictly adaptive in so many cases that botanists
now believe that all the external characters of
flowers either are or have been of use to the
species." Wallace delights to trace such use,
and has illustrated very specially three useful
agencies employed in the development of plants
and animals.

II.

THE MEANS OF SCATTERING SEEDS AND FER-
TILIZING PLANTS.—Some of these have been
noticed with wonder and admiration from ancient date. Seeds are carried by winds all
around, sometimes to immense distances, perhaps hundreds of miles. They have been
transported across seas, on rare occasions from
one hemisphere to another. Often the seeds
are downy, so that they are easily wafted
through the air. We have all observed that
some of them have curious hooks to attach
them to objects, or they possess adhesive matter whereby to cling to positions where they can
germinate.

But of late years attention has been called to
a very curious means of propagating plants.
Birds and insects, such as bees, wasps, and but-

terflies, dip into flowers and fruits for nectar, honey, and other kinds of food, and as they do so the pollen adheres to them and they bear it to other plants, which they fertilize. It is pleasant to see the insects flitting from flower to flower, sipping sweets for themselves; but our pleasure is increased when we find them at the same time carrying on unconsciously a work necessary for the preservation of the economy of Nature. Some plants are self-propagating and do not need the aid of these carriers; but others have no means of self-fertilizing, and are dependent for the continuance of the species on the creatures which feed upon them, and are busy, without their meaning or knowing it, in carrying the fertilizing power from plant to plant. Naturalists tell us that plants generally are benefited by cross fertilizing; it is in this way that new forms of beauty are produced, as we see in roses, in pansies, and innumerable plants in our gardens, in the fields, and on the mountains. This work is conducted largely by birds, butterflies, and flying insects, which thus make plants fulfil their offices and cover the earth, to give animals their food and show their beauty to man, if he will only appreciate it.

III.

Mimicry a Means of Preserving Plants
and Animals.—This is a very curious subject.
Naturalists have been led to take special notice
of it of late years. Edible animals and plants
liable to be attacked as prey take the form of
inedible creatures which devouring birds and
insects are careful to avoid. Wasps and bees,
which can defend themselves by their stings,
are often imitated by insects of other orders,
which are thus saved from destruction. Certain harmless snakes mimic poisonous species,
and are thus preserved. A butterfly has been
known to take the form of a snake with a threat-
ening aspect, and thus it frightens its foes. It
is said that the Kallima butterfly of India, as
it rests on a twig, can scarcely be distinguished
from a colored leaf. The British cuckoo is a
very defenceless bird, but in color and markings is much like a sparrow-hawk, and is, therefore, not likely to be attacked. Let us understand precisely what these provisions mean.
They amount to this, that defenceless creatures
are more apt to be preserved by their resem-
bling others which, as known to be able to
meet their assailants, are not apt to be assailed.
It does look as if the species which have this

property of mimicking are more likely to be
preserved in the struggle for existence and go
down to future generations. The most remarkable cases are those which are protected
by color, and instances will be given under the
next head.

IV.

COLOR AS A MEANS OF RECOGNITION AND
PROTECTION.—Color in the animal kingdom is
an influential means of recognition, perhaps
more than even form. It is by its marking
and its hues that animals readily recognize
their kin of the same species, that the bird
discovers its mate, that the female spies the
male. Some birds will not pair with a bird of
a different color, even though it be of its own
species. There are special " markings, bands,
spots or patches of white or of bright color
which vary in every species—and are often
concealed when the creature is at rest, but dis-
played when in motion—as in the case of the
bands and spots so frequent on the wings and
tails of birds. Now these specific markings are
believed, with good reason, to serve the purpose of enabling each species to be quickly
recognized, even at a distance, by its fellows,
especially the parents by their young, and the

two sexes by each other ; and this recognition must often be an important factor in securing the safety of individuals, and therefore the well-being and continuance of the species." Wallace adds : " The most common of all the characters by which species are distinguished from each other, their colors and markings can be shown to be adaptive or utilitarian." He is inclined to think that easy recognition " has had a more widespread influence in determining the diversities of animal coloration than any other cause whatever."

Color is a means of protection. Some colors are attractive and draw attention to the plant or animal, others are a warning or a signal flag against attack. Birds, butterflies, and insects are apt to take the color of the ground or food on which they live. Birds in the arctic regions are commonly white, so that they are concealed in the snow. The raven in the same region retains its black color because it is "a powerful bird and fears no enemy, while being a carrion feeder it has no need for concealment in order to approach its prey." In the rich vegetation of the tropics many birds, such as parrots and paroquets, are apt to take a green color, and so are not distinguishable. But as they need to be discerned by their mates, birds in tropical forests have usually small but brilliant patches of color. The pale color of birds prevalent in sandy and arid districts is in harmony with the general tints of the surface.   In the case of many birds the eggs are so like the surroundings that it is difficult to distinguish them at any distance. In decaying vegetation the eggs are apt to be spotted, but not brilliantly.   Those who hunt tigers and panthers tell us that it is often difficult to see them at any distance in the midst of the grass and under the trees. Wallace says the earliest leaf-eating insects acquired a green color as one of the necessaries of their existence.   Those feeding on particular species would speedily acquire the peculiar tints and markings best adapted to conceal them upon these plants.   We have all noticed how insects are apt to take the colors of the plants on which they feed. "It seems not improbable that fully one-half of the species in the animal kingdom possess colors which have been more or less adapted to secure for them conceal-. ment or protection."

It is of vast importance, in order to preserve the species, that birds should be protected while hatching. From our childhood we have been interested to observe how this has been effected by their nests, often curiously constructed, being concealed in thick foliage or in holes. But there is another very powerful provision to secure the same end: while the male has often a showy coloring to attract the female, the female has often a tamer color to keep her unobserved. There are cases in which the male has the plainer coloring, but in these he sits on the eggs and the female fights the battles.

We could mention vast numbers of different kinds of color-concealment, but it will suffice to specify only a few. There are birds which lay their white eggs in open nests.

"All the duck tribe, the grebes, and the pheasants belong to this class; but these birds all have the habit of covering their eggs with dead leaves or other material whenever they leave the nests, so as effectually to conceal them. Other birds, as the short-eared owl, the goat-sucker, the partridge, and some of the Australian ground pigeons, lay their white or pale eggs on the bare soil, but in these cases the birds themselves are protectively colored, so that when sitting they are almost invisible,

and they have the habit of sitting close and
almost continually, thus concealing their eggs.
Pigeons and doves offer a very curious case of
the protection of exposed eggs.   They usually
build very slight and loose nests of sticks and
twigs, so open that light can be seen through
them from below, while they are generally well
concealed by foliage from above.   Their eggs
are white and shining; yet it is a difficult matter to discover from beneath whether there are
eggs in the nest or not, while they are well
hidden by the thick foliage above."

Briefly: " The white of arctic animals, the
yellowish tint of the desert forms, the dusky
hues of crepuscular and nocturnal species, the
transparent or bluish tints of oceanic creatures, represent a vast host in themselves; but
we have an equally numerous body whose tints
are adapted to tropical foliage, to the bark of
trees, or to the soil, or to the dead leaves, on or
among which they habitually live.   Then we
have innumerable special adaptations to the
tints and forms of leaves or twigs or flowers;
to bark or moss, to rock or pebble, by which
such vast numbers of the insect tribes obtain
protection ; and we have seen that these various forms of coloration are equally prevalent

in the waters of the seas and the oceans, and
are thus co-extensive with the domains of life
upon the earth."

Mr. Darwin first stated that flowers had
been rendered conspicuous in order to attract
insects which carry the seeds to fertilize plants.
If insects had not been developed on the
earth our plants would not have been decked
with beautiful flowers, but would have produced only such poor flowers as we see in our
fir, oak, and ash trees, on grasses, docks, and
nettles, which are all fertilized by the agency
of the wind.

V.

PROFESSOR DRUMMOND'S TROPICAL AFRICA.
—In this work we have very interesting illustrations of the ends accomplished by the
adaptations of color and forms. In some cases
these serve the purposes of protection, in
others of warning. Birds, monkeys, lizards,
and spiders are very fond of butterflies. But
there are two great families of butterflies, the
Danaides and *Acraiedæ*, which are inedible
owing to the presence in their bodies of acrid
and unwholesome juices, and so they are saved
from attack. They are distinguished by loud
patterns and brilliant colorings, and float with-

out danger the forests with the utmost coolness
in the broadest daylight with leisureliness, de-
fiance, and self-complacency, while their duskier
brethren have to hurry through the glades in
terror of their lives. For the same reason,
well-armed or stinging insects are always con-
spicuously ornamented with warning colors.
"The expense of eating a wasp, for instance,
is too great to lead to a second investment in
the same insect, and wasps, therefore, have been
rendered as showy as possible, so that they
may be at once seen and carefully avoided.
The same law applies to bees, dragon-flies, and
other gaudy forms ; and it may be taken as a
rule that all gayly-colored insects belong to
one or other of these two classes ; that is,
they are either bad eating or bad stingers.
Now the remarkable fact is that all these brilliant and unwholesome creatures are closely
imitated in outward apparel by other creatures
not themselves protected by acrid juices, but
which thus share the same immunity."

The puff adder is from three to five feet
long and very thick, is ornamented with strange
devices in green, yellow, and black. Its true
habitat is among fallen leaves in the deep
shade of the trees by the banks of the streams.

Now in such a position at the distance of a foot
or two its appearance so exactly resembles the
forest bed as to be almost indistinguishable
from it. The harmony of color with environment is often very striking, even among large
animals. "When we look, for instance, at
the coat of a zebra with thunder-and-lightning
pattern of black and white stripes, we should
think such a conspicuous object designed to
court rather than to elude attention. But the
effect in nature is just the opposite. The
black and white somehow take away the sense
of a solid body altogether. The two colors
seem to blend into the most inconspicuous
gray, and at close quarters the effect is of bars
of light seen through the branches of shrubs."
The spotted pelt probably conveys the same
sense of indistinctness, as in the case of the
zebra. "The crocodile is marvellously concealed by its knotted and mud-covered hide,
and it is often quite impossible to tell at a
distance whether the objects lying along the
river banks are alligators or fallen logs."

The most remarkable cases are those which
have both form and color employed as mimicry.
The mantis and locust tribes are found in all
forms, sizes, and colors mimicking foliage at

every stage of growth, maturity, and decay. "Some have the leaf stamped on their broadened wing-cases in vivid green, with veins and midrib complete, and with curious expansions over the thorax and along all the limbs to imitate smaller leaves. I have again and again matched these forms in the forest, not only with the living leaf, but with crumpled, discolored, and shrivelled specimens ; and the imitations of the crumpled autumn leaf are even more numerous and impressive than those of the living form. Lichens, mosses, and fungi are also taken as models by insects, and there is probably nothing in the vegetal kingdom, no knot, wart, nut, mould, scale, bract, thorn, or bark, which has not its living counterpart in some animal form.   Most of the moths, beetles, weevils, and especially the larval forms, are more or less protected mimetically ; and, in fact, almost the entire population of the tropics is guilty of personation in ways known or unknown. The lichen-mimicking insects even go the length of imitating holes, by means of mirror-like pools of black, irregularly disposed on the backs, or interrupting the otherwise dangerous symmetry of the fringed sides."

There are insects which imitate twigs, sticks, and the smaller branches of shrubs. There is the walking twig, three or four inches long, covered with bark apparently and spotted all over with mould like the genuine branch. " On finding one of these insects I have often cut a small branch from an adjoining tree, and laid the two side by side for comparison, and when both are partly concealed by the hands, so as to show only the part of the insect's body which is free from limbs, it is impossible to tell the one from the other. The very joints of the legs in these forms are knobbed to represent nodes, and the characteristic attitudes of the insects are such as to sustain the deception."

One of the most striking illustrations is exhibited by the grass-stalk insects which live in long grass all over the forest. " When you catch him his limbs are twisted about at every angle, as if the whole were made of one long stalk of the most delicate grass hinged in a dozen places, and then gently crushed up into a dishevelled heap. Having once assumed a position by a wonderful in-stinct, he never moves or varies one of his many angles by half a degree." " To complete the deception, some have the antennae developed to represent blades of grass, which are often from one to two inches in length, and stick out from the end of the body, one on either side, like blades of grass at the end of a stalk. The favorite attitude of these insects is to grasp a grass-stalk, as if they were climbing a pole ; then the body is compressed against the stem, and held in position by the two fore-limbs which are extended in front, so as to form one long line with the body, and so mixed up with the stalk, as to be practically part of it. The four legs stand out anyhow in rigid spikes like forks from the grass, while the antennæ are erected at the top, like blades coming off from a node, which the button-like head so well resembles. When one of these insects springs to a new stalk, it will at once all but vanish before our eyes. It remains there perfectly rigid a component part of the grass itself, its long legs crooked and branched exactly like dried hay, the same in color, the same in fitness, and quite defying detection." During three-fourths of the year the grass is dried by the sun into a straw-yellow color, and all the insects are painted to match. Although yellow is the ground tone of these grasses, they are variegated, and especially towards the latter half the year, in two ways. They are either tinged here and there with red and brown like the autumn colors, or they are streaked and spotted with black or other markings painted by the finger of decay. All these appearances are closely imitated by insects. The blades alike with limbs, and are variously colored according to season and habitat.

VI.

EFFICIENT WITH FINAL CAUSE.—These run through the whole of nature. They have been known to have been different since the days of Aristotle, who distinguished them, and yet they are connected. When we use a magnet we are employing efficient cause. When we join other things with it to form a compass we have final cause, an end to serve by agents. We have seen that there are adaptations implying a purpose, but there must also be agents producing them. Whether we are able to discover them or not, there must be powers causing the adaptive colors and forms which we discover in nature. Wallace does not always distinguish between the two kinds of causes. In his explanations Wallace often writes as if he had found an efficient, when he has only observed a final cause. Following physicists generally, he regards color as altogether subjective. In this I think he is mistaken. Color, like heat, which is a mode of motion, is an external cause of an organic affection. As such it has an objective existence. I do not say what precise sort of existence. I believe it exists, as a power or powers. According to the doctrine of Newton, when the white beam strikes on a plant it is divided into two parts, one part is reflected by the color of the surface, and the other is absorbed. While taken into the plant it is not lost—according to the doctrine of the conservation of energy no force is ever lost. It may abide for a time in the plant, till it is changed into some other form. Being in the plant, it is apt to come out in a complementary color, that is, in colors which together make up the white beam. Such colors are said to be in harmony, and when under the eyes at the same time are felt to be agreeable to man, and probably also to some or many of the lower animals.

We discover these complementary colors appearing together in nature. Thus we have green harmonizing with red and russet. The

soft hue which the author of nature has given to
the leaf of tree and herbage is by far the most
abundant color in the vegetable kingdom.
Now, wherever the flower of a plant is red it
associates agreeably with the leaf. The flowers
of the rose and of many pinks, geraniums, mal-
lows, lychnises, and innumerable others contrast strikingly with the foliage of the plants
on which they grow. The eye delights to see
the fruit of the cherry, the rose, and the thorn,
and the berry of the holly, the yew, the common
barberry, the mountain ash, and many others
peeping forth from the green leaves. It often
happens that according to the green so is the
hue of the associated red. Again there is purple harmonizing with yellow and citrine. Purple of various tints, shades, and hues, such as
red purple where there is a preponderance of
red, and blue-purple where there is a predom-
inance of blue, is the most frequent color
of the petals of plants, and in beautiful contrast we often find yellow in the centre of the
flower. Thus in the garden polyanthus,
and in many varieties of auricula, the outer
rim of the corolla is purple and an inner cir-
cle is yellow. More frequently the comple-
ment is found in the yellow anthers or yellow

pollen. It is certainly a noteworthy circumstance that as the frequent color of petals is
purple so the most common color of the pollen
of plants is yellow.   In the flower of the for-
get-me-not which ever greets the eye so cheer-
ily there is a border of blue purple and a centre or throat of orange yellow.   In the pansy
so rich and soft we have yellow of various hues
and degrees of intensity brightened by a mixture of white. Eyebright has a purple and
white corolla with a sprinkling of yellow on its
odd lobe.

These harmonies prevail in other departments.   In the evening sky the beam is divided
into two, and we gaze on the blue or blue
purple cloud contrasted with varied hues of
red orange.   Shells are commonly yellow, with
purple spots decorating them.   In birds we
have commonly a sort of tawny hue, being a
yellow with more or less of red, and a dark
blue, or rather a dark blue purple. This collocation of colors is very frequent among our
domestic fowls (the cock struts so magnifi-
cently amidst an immense profusion of purple
and gold) and among raptorial birds, as for
example, many falcons and owls, and is found
among wading birds and many species of

thrushes. In more ornamented birds we discover red associated with green as in a number of todies and a great many parrots.

These harmonies make the objects of nature interesting and attractive to man, possibly also to animals. Acting with them is the beneficent principle of natural selection, which serves specially to furnish recognition, warning, and protection. But there are always agencies at work which produce these effects. Wallace shows that colors are most apt to come out on the parts of the plant and animal in which there is the most active vitality—the vitality commonly chemical action, drawing the color absorbed in the plant towards the part. "Color has arisen over surfaces where muscular and nervous development is considerable." The crown of the head, the throat, the ear-coverts, the eyes; the plumes have usually distinct tints in high-colored birds.

We have seen that animals are apt to take the color of the ground on which they lie. Of course they feed on that ground, and the color may be produced by the food on which they live, and by the survival of the fittest. There must also be a cause of the form of mimicry which they take; this may be found in part in

the tendencies of the animal and plant to take
the same forms, as for instance, both to produce joints.

In this chapter I have simply opened up a
new and interesting field. Others will enter in
and possess it.   It must evidently be the main
topic of discussion in the Theology of Nature
in the age to which we have come.

CHAPTER VI.

GEOLOGY AND SCRIPTURE.

I.

HARMONY OF GENESIS AND GEOLOGY.—It is not necessary to dwell on this subject. The correspondence has been demonstrated of late years by very competent men whose writings are accessible to all. In particular this has been done by the three men on this continent who have the best right to speak on this subject from their knowledge of physical geography and geology,—Dr. Guyot, Dr. Dana, and Sir William Dawson. I have been most indebted to the late Dr. Guyot's little book on "Creation."

In the one of these, the written record, we have an account of the genesis of the earth as it would have been witnessed by a spectator who had lived through the unremembered ages ; in the other the combined results of the researches of geologists within the last few ages. The one is ocular ; the other scientific.

This accounts at once for their essential sameness and their superficial differences—which do not imply any contradiction. Professor Huxley showed in a lecture in New York that there were contradictions between geology and Milton's picture of creation in " Paradise Lost," but he made no special reference to the Bible account—we may believe out of reverence—and he did not attempt to prove that geology contradicted Genesis.[1]

I believe that if you would ask a geologist to write for us a true account of the production of our earth in as brief a space as the first chapter of our Bible, he would confess his inability to do so. Suppose that the opening chapter of Genesis, all unknown before, were discovered and published in our day, it would at once be denounced as a forgery, constructed by one who knows geological science, and who varies the record simply to keep the trick from being detected.

---

[1] Elsewhere in his reply to Gladstone he alleges that the Bible errs in placing birds earlier than reptiles. This he does by making (Gen. i., 24) "creeping thing" mean reptile, whereas I understand by it the lower mammals. Reptiles being mostly amphibious, are included in *taninnim* (Gen. i., 21), the moving or winged creatures placed before birds. In these ages there were numbers of flying creatures, including not only reptiles but amphibians.

II.

THE CORRESPONDENCE.—It consists first in both arranging the history into progressive periods in the one called Days, in the other Ages, Epochs, Formations; secondly, in the order of the appearance of living beings; and thirdly, in man being the consummation of the whole.

It may be useful to preface the comparison with a statement by Dana as to the geological epochs. "First, the reality of an age in history is marked by the development of some new idea in the system of progress; secondly, the beginning of the characteristics of an age may be looked for in the midst of a preceding age, and the marks of the future coming out to view are prophetic of the future" ("Geol.," p. 137).

It is scarcely necessary to show, after it has been so often done, that the word "Day" is constantly used in Scripture to designate a fixed period of any kind and is not confined to a period of 24 hours. Indeed, it is applied in Chapter i. of Genesis to the first three days, when, as yet, the sun was not formed and there could not have been days as we now measure them. In Genesis ii., 4, Moses writes " in the day," (the meaning being a period—a very lengthened one,) "that the Lord God made the earth and the heavens." So it goes on in nearly every book of Scripture. It has been counted that there are upwards of a hundred places in which the phrase denotes a period other than that of the rotation of the earth.

We may now compare and contrast the two accounts the record by the spectator, and that by the savant. I keep to the general correspondence, which is sufficient for my purpose, and do not specify minute points about which there may be differences of interpretation.

It should be observed that in both there is an antecedent and unknown period, when, according to Genesis, the earth was without form and void; when there was a deep with darkness upon it, and when, according to geology, the mundane matter was shapeless and without life. The days or epochs begin with the creative acts.

GENESIS.   GEOLOGY.

FIRST DAY.

The Spirit, the source of power and order, moves on the deep, and there is light.	There is no formed sun, but there is light ready to germinate the life now to appear.

SECOND DAY.

The separation of the now sol-	The consolidation of the earth

idified earth from the expanse of heaven above.

from its previous igneous state, and the separation of the earth from its gaseous environment.

THIRD DAY.

The dry land appears above the waters which previously covered it, and thus early plant-life appears.

There is vegetable life of a simple form anticipated in the Eozoic period, and coming forth more fully in the Silurian period.

FOURTH DAY.[1]

The sun, moon, and stars become visible, and henceforth rule the seasons.

In this era the sun is formed into a definite shape, the moon is thrown off from the earth, and the stars become visible, owing to the atmosphere being cleared.

FIFTH DAY.

Creation of the lower animals in water and in air. " And God said, let the waters teem with creeping things, swarm with swarmers, and fowl that may fly above the earth. And God created the great stretched out sea monsters (tanninim), and all living creatures that creep, which the waters breed abundantly after their kind, and every winged bird after its kind."

There are the lower forms of animals, chiefly marine, fishes, reptiles, rising to fowls. The latter part of the Palæozoic and the Mesozoic ages.

---

[1] I remember that when I was a boy an old infidel addressed me : " Oh, how can you believe the Bible, which says there was light before the sun appeared ? " I was not able to answer the objection, but science now can do so when it tells us that the formed earth is older than the formed sun, and that there must have been light nourishing plants before the sun was condensed. In the present advanced stage of science, the infidel would have started an objection which cannot be answered if Genesis had made the sun appear on the first day.

SIXTH DAY.

Higher animals appear, carnivorous, herbivorous, smaller mammalia. such as rats, mice, and emphatically man, who has dominion over all animals. He is made in the image of God.

It is the age of mammals including marsupials. It culminates in man, who is in all points a mammal, but has intelligence, reason, and moral perception, as testified by psychology—a branch of science as certain as geology.

III.

HOW IS THE CORRESPONDENCE TO BE ACCOUNTED FOR?—The question arises and demands an answer, How comes it that there is such a correspondence between Genesis and Science, which has been formed in so much a later age? According to the common reckoning, which can be justified, the Pentateuch was written by Moses 1400 years before the Christian era. The wildest German neologists are sure it could not have been written later than the time of Ezra, 500 years before Christ. Every one ackowledges that the Pentateuch was translated into Greek between 300 and 200 years B. C., and that after this copies of it were to be found in many libraries. How, then, were the early Scriptures able to publish truths which have only been discovered by science in this century; truths many and varied and minute, and covering a lengthened series of years, amounting to at least a hundred millions?

There is only one answer to which reason will listen for an instant—the truths must have been disclosed to Moses as they profess by the immediate inspiration of God.

Those who do not believe in the inspiration of the ancient record have great difficulty in answering the question. Thus Dr. Romanes admits that "the order in which the flora and fauna are said by the Mosaic account to have appeared upon the earth corresponds with that which the theory of evolution requires and the evidence of geology proves."[1] He is able in explanation only to say, that "the grand old legend may contain in its beautiful allegory more of traditional history than the present age is always inclined to suppose." Tradition of whom? Of brutes who leave no record behind them, except their bones to geologists? Of men who have not got the science to hand down? Haeckel seems to take pleasure in declaring: "Two great and fundamental ideas, common also to the non-miraculous, meet us in the Mosaic hypothesis of creation with surprising clearness and simplicity—the idea of separation or differentiation, and the idea of progressive development or perfecting. Al-

---

[1] *Nature*, August, 1881.

though Moses looks upon the results of the
great laws of organic development which we
shall later point out, as the necessary conclu-
sions of the Doctrine of Descent, as the direct
actions of a constructing creator, yet in this
theory there lies hidden the ruling idea of a
progressive development and differentiation of
the originally simple matter. We can therefore bestow our just and sincere admiration of
the Jewish law-giver's grand insight into nature." [1]   But the statement of Moses does not
consist of an "idea," or "a grand insight," but
of a long and detailed series of events such as
could only have been discovered by scientific
observation, and such as could not have been
discovered by observation at the time of Moses.
Even an Aristotle, a Newton, or a Cuvier, could
not have constructed, by natural science, a cos-
mology, such as is presented to us in Genesis,
had they lived 1400 years before Christ.   I am
not sure that Moses had such a grand insight
into nature as Haeckel gives him credit for, or
even understood fully what he wrote, of which
we are constrained to seek the producing power
in an inspiration from on high.

<hr>

[1] Haeckel's "History of Creation," vol. i., p. 38.

CHAPTER VII.

THE AGE OF MAN.

FIRST EPOCH, THAT OF STRUGGLE.

I.

THE COMING TIME.—In all the geological ages we find in any one age the anticipation of the following. This may also be the case with the age in which we now live, the Age of Man. We see everywhere preparations made for further progress : seeds sown which have not yet sprung up ; embryos not yet developed ; life which has not yet grown to maturity. In particular we find that in this Age of Man, man has not yet completed his work.

In an age there is often more than one Epoch ; thus, we have the Lower and Upper Silurian ; in the Mesozoic, the Triassic, Jurassic, and Cretaceous. So in this Human Age we find two very marked Epochs, that of labor and that of rest, that of battle and of victory. The evening and the morning constitute the seventh as they do the other days.

II.

Man's Descent.—We have to answer the
question so often put : Did man come into the
world by ordinary generation? Of course,
from the lower animals? To this I answer
that at first sight there is something special in
the forthcoming of man, and this conviction is
deepened the deeper we explore his nature, his
intellectual, moral, and spiritual faculties, his
reason, his conscience, his free-will, which raise
him far above the brutes. Your one-eyed evolutionists see only one side, and not the whole
solid truth. Man is undoubtedly an animal;
this of the highest, the mammalian form, the
mammal standing upright and looking to
heaven. But he is higher than the animal, and
is allied to God, who made him and made all
things. He discerns between truth and error,
between good and evil; he sees distant conse-
quences, and can rise to spiritual communion
with God.

This is the double account of man given in
Scripture. In Genesis i., he is higher than
the animals, and has dominion over them ; he
is made in the image of God. This of his
soul. In Genesis ii., he is formed of " the
dust of the ground." But there is a higher

power superinduced ; God "breathed into his nostrils the breath of life, and he became a living soul." We have a most inadequate view of the nature of man unless we look at both these aspects. The anatomist, the materialist, does not see half the man. His microscope may show us the soft pulpy nerves and brain, but cannot exhibit to us the soul with its high imaginings, its lofty perceptions, its sense of moral obligation, its glimpses of the world to come.

Mr. Alfred B. Wallace, the co-discoverer with Darwin of universal evolution, argues that there is something special in man's appearance on the earth. It is not a development from what existed before; it is a creation of something new; a capacity of beholding, admiring, and following the good, the holy. But this new power is not altogether an anomaly, an exception. It is one of a series, the highest of the series. We have seen that rising above matter there is life, there is feeling, there is intelligence, there is moral discernment, and now there is love and law; there is love to expand and law to bind the universe. If any one ask me if I believe man's body to have come from a brute, I answer that I know not. I believe in revelation, I believe in science, but neither has revealed this to me ; and I restrain the weak curiosity which would tempt me to inquire into what cannot be known. Meanwhile I am sure, and I assert, that man's soul is of a higher origin and of a nobler type.

III.

THE WARFARE.—Scientific men have now hit on the fit phrase, "the struggle for existence," which so aptly characterizes our era. In books on natural theology, writen in the last century and the beginning of this, this world was pictured as a scene of order and beauty, of wisdom and benevolence. Now the picture has been darkened. It is seen and acknowledged that if there be good in our world, there is also evil. We have as clear and decided proof of the existence of the one as of the other. There is pain in our world, and this is certainly an evil ; pain to which we are all liable, often keen and long continued, lasting for hours, and days, and years, without the possibility of alleviation, and the sufferer has to cry in the evening, when shall it be morning, and in the morning, when shall it be evening. There is the deeper evil, apparently the source of all other evils—that of sin, of ingratitude, lust, deceit, malignity. We feel it in ourselves, we take guilt to ourselves, being convicted by our own consciences. No explanation, no history of our world is at all adequate to explain the facts, unless it looks at both these aspects, the evil and the good. In the very midst of our world is the tree of knowledge of good and evil; as in the midst of the paradise restored is the tree of life.

The history of our world is given in epitome, Gen. iii., 15: "I will put enmity between thee and the woman, and between thy seed and her seed; it shall bruise thy head and thou shalt bruise his heel." The contest is between the good, represented by the seed of the woman,—not "seeds," as of many, but seed, as of one, the deliverer,—and the seed of the serpent; in which contest the seed of the woman, bitten in the heel, shall bruise the head of the serpent and crush the evil. This world is not a scene of pure good or of unmixed evil: it is one of contest between the evil and the good; between the seed of the serpent, the animal and the malignant power, and the seed of the woman, the pure and the loving power. We have an emblem of it in the Tree of Life, allowed for a time in the

garden of Eden, and the flaming sword burning every way to guard it. We have it exhibited in Cain slaying his brother Abel; "and
wherefore slew he him? because his own
works were evil and his brother's righteous."
We see it in the two families which divided
the antediluvian world, that of Cain and that of
Seth. Many of the Psalms, which the Church
continues to sing, as they are in accordance
with the experience of our hearts, are war
songs: "Gird thy sword upon thy thigh, O
Most Mighty, and in thy majesty ride prosper-
ously, because of truth and meekness and
righteousness, and thy right hand shall teach
thee terrible things." Psalms xlv., 3, 4.
The burden of the prophets is deliverance from
evil. " He shall see of the travail of his soul,
and shall be satisfied." Throughout the dis-
courses of our Lord there is reference to the
good contending with the evil and overcoming
it. The tares sown by the enemy grow with
the wheat until the harvest, when the tares are
burnt. The essence of the Gospel is to be
found in the lost sheep brought back by the
shepherd, in the lost money found, in the lost
son in the embraces of his father. The warfare is not only without us, the deeper struggle

is within. " The flesh lusteth against the spirit
and the spirit against the flesh, and they are
contrary the one to the other." The whole
warfare is described in Romans vii., 8–25.
" I see a law of my members warring against
a law of my mind." " O wretched man that I
am! who shall deliver me from the body of this
death?" " I thank God through Jesus Christ
our Lord." The decisive battle was fought
when Jesus suffered on the cross ; the victory
was won when he rose from the dead and as-
cended into heaven leading captivity captive.

SECOND EPOCH; THE SPIRITUAL.

IV.

THE REDEMPTION.—God is love ; essentially
love. He loves every living creature as if he
were the only one whom he loved ; he cares
for the lilies of the field and the fowls of
heaven, for the widows and the fatherless. I
believe that in every one of the countless
worlds, counted only by him who counts the
number of the stars, there may be a separate
manifestation of the manifold wisdom of God.
I am sure that each of the worlds has es-
pecial marks of his love. One of the highest is in that world in which we dwell, the

world which has fallen, the world that has sinned, but which he redeems and restores. I am not sure that there is a higher, that there can be a higher. "When the fulness of time was come 'God sent forth his Son, made of a woman, made under the law to redeem them that were under the law, that we might receive the adoption of sons" (Gal. iv., 4). Here in the world in which we dwell the Creator has become the creature to associate himself more intimately with creation. "The Logos was made flesh, and dwelt among us" (John i., 14). Though fully and altogether man, he does not become so by ordinary generation ; he is born of a virgin. There is a fixed time, a fit time, in his coming, and in all the events of his life, which cannot be delayed nor hastened. There are sin and suffering in our world, and the Son of God became man that he might suffer in our room and stead, and sin is atoned for while it is condemned. This was planned and contemplated from the beginning. He is "the lamb slain from the foundation of the world." (Rev. xiii., 8). I was set up from everlasting, from the beginning, or ever the earth was." "He was rejoicing in his habitable earth [new version], and his delights were with

the sons of men." (Prov. viii., 23, 31). Who
is this that cometh from afar, "with dyed gar-
ments?" "This that is glorious in his apparel,
travelling in the greatness of his strength? I
that speak in righteousness, mighty to save"
(Is. lxiii., 1). "He was wounded for our trans-
gressions; he was bruised for our iniquities."
(Is. liii., 5). He has become perfect through
suffering (Heb. ii., 10). To perfect his love he
suffered, that the love of benevolence might
also become the love of sympathy; he feels for
us, for he has felt with us.

V.

SIGNS OF RESTORATION.—There is certainly
evil in our world, but there is also good. The
scene is a chequered one of light and shadow.
We live in a world where day and night alter-
nate. Every man walks in light, but accom-
panied by his own shadow, the shadow being
sin, which is the obstruction offered to the light.
But the creature is striving against the tendency
to evil. If there be diseases in our world, there
are also remedies. If there be winters in the
succession of seasons, there are also springs
going on to summers and harvests. If there
be the death of the individual, there is a continuance of the race. If there be deaths, there

are also resurrections. Nature is struggling, but it is in order to improvement. It is plough-ing and sowing, but in order to reap in due season. It is moving onward, but also upward. It is groaning, but it is to be delivered from a load. It is travailing, but it is for a birth. It is not perfect, but it is going on toward perfection.

Looking to our earth, we find causes working which will certainly improve it. Education has reached a high state in certain countries, and will spread to all by missions and other agencies, thereby stimulating intelligence. Agriculture is advancing, and will destroy wild beasts, culti-vate wastes, and spread fertility. Commerce is binding the nations closer together. Human life is being lengthened indefinitely. "The child shall die a hundred years old."

The Scriptures all along look forward to a better era. The seed of the woman is to bruise the serpent's head. In Abraham's seed all the nations of the earth are to be blessed. The Psalms commonly begin with praise, describe a fight, and close with a triumph. The prophets look forward to a light about to dawn, and their faces are brightened by it. "And it shall come to pass afterward, that I will pour out my spirit on all flesh" (Joel ii., 28).

VI.

THE DISPENSATION OF THE SPIRIT.—A new
power is imparted, and begins to work. "The
spirit of the Lord is upon me, because he hath
anointed me to preach the gospel to the poor;
He hath sent me to heal the broken-hearted,
to preach deliverance to the captives, and re-
covering of sight to the blind, to set at liberty
them that are bruised, to preach the acceptable
year of the Lord" (Luke iv., 18, 19), the year
of jubilee, the year of restoration.

The king establishes a kingdom. On leaving the earth, he leaves one to carry on the
work. "I will send another Comforter, to abide
with you forever, even the Spirit of Truth"
(John xiv., 16, 17). "Thus spake he of the
Spirit, which they that believe on him should
receive" (John vii., 39). But while travailing on earth, he had to say The Holy Ghost
was not yet given, because that Jesus was not
yet glorified (John vii., 39). In a sense, the
Holy Ghost was given before, and had fallen
on one after another in the Old Testament
times, perhaps also on such men as Socrates
(who claimed to have been guided by a dai-
monion) in other lands. But this was an anticipation; as we have seen that in geological

times a higher life would appear in an earlier than its own proper age—the mammal in the age of reptiles. The new power descended when "the day of Pentecost," the feast of first fruits was " fully come" (Luke ii., 1). A new epoch has begun. For a time there is a struggle between the flesh and the spirit.

We have seen that when the new powers come in they act upon, and act with the old. The organic, as the higher, employs the inorganic powers, which, in spite of resistance, it turns to its own uses. Intelligence, instinctive and rational, directs and controls both, and morality would turn them all to a high end. It is thus, also, with the development now going on. It proceeds by two potencies, the natural and the spiritual. As I have said elsewhere: " There are the old powers still working, those of sense and understanding, of reason and conscience. These constitute the life which God breathed into man when he became a living soul. Their crowning part is the reason, speculative and moral, made after the likeness of God, and lying deep down in our nature, beneath the incrustations covering it from the sight, but capable of being wakened up. Upon these the new and spiritual powers work. Much that takes place in the Church is the joint result of the two. The inspiration of Moses, of the prophets, and apostles, did not destroy their natural character; it merely sanctified and elevated them. The spirits of the prophets were subject to them. Religion does not eradicate the natural powers, it moulds them and directs them to higher ends. The man's faculties and temperament are not changed by his being converted; if he was lively and impulsive before, he is so still, if dull and solid, he will continue to be so; but the whole elevated by the spiritual power."

In all past ages there have been new powers added. Life seized on the mineral mass, and formed the plant; sensation imparted to the plant made the animal; instinct has preserved the life and elevated it; intelligence has turned the animal into man; morality has raised the intelligence to love and law. The work of the Spirit is not an anomaly. It is one of a series; the last and the highest. It is the grandest of all the powers. It is an inward power, convincing, converting, sanctifying, beautifying, and preparing the soul for a heavenly rest, where, however, "they rest not day nor night"; for rest consists in holy and blessed service.

The history of our earth is thus one, a connected and consistent whole—a system. It is a struggle and a victory. Our older divines used to argue that death came on the lower animals because of the sin of Adam. Geology has dissipated this fancy, which has no countenance in Scripture, and has shown us that death has reigned from the beginning of life " over them that had not sinned after the similitude of Adam's transgression, who is the figure of him that was to come," who has gone down into the grave, grappled with death, and conquered it.

Our lot has been cast in the time of war. " Woe is me that I dwell in Mesech "—the scene of strife. But all the while, thanks be to God, who hath called me to be a soldier with the whole armor of God at my command, and sure of victory. I am but a common soldier in the heart of the battle, and I see but a little way around me. But I see in front of me the captain of my salvation leading, and I follow him. Already in anticipation I hear the shout of victory. " Blessing and honor and glory and power be unto him that sitteth upon the throne and unto the lamb for ever and ever."

There has been a troubled day, but "at

evening time there is light." Every mystery
is cleared up ; every evil is removed ; the
last enemy is destroyed ; death is swallowed
up in victory ; the conqueror has gone up on
high. " Lift up your heads, O ye gates ; even
lift them up, ye everlasting doors, and the king
of glory shall enter in." It is revealed that the
saints shall live and reign with him " a thousand years " (Rev. xx.,4), the day standing for a
year, and constituting a geological epoch.

VII.

THE CLOSE.—I have tried to unfold a pan-
orama of our earth's history, from its com-
mencement to its close, so far as I can see it
by the light of science and of Scripture. It is
a flickering light, with crossings and interferences of rays. At times I am dazzled with
excess of light, and at times there is a dimness
by reason of distance, and I can scarcely distinguish land from cloud. The several Ages
rise like mountain ranges, one beyond the
other, apt to be covered with clouds, but their
outlines visible one beyond the other, with val-
leys between. The history is one throughout,
the evening and the morning always making
the day.

In the dim distance I see the scene of darkness, with unending light beyond.		After the thousand years are fulfilled, Satan—that is, the power of evil—must be loosed for à little while (Rev. xx., 3).		It is a brief, it is the final, conquest.		"There came down fire from heaven and destroyed them."		It is a curious and most noteworthy circumstance, that according to recent science if the powers in nature continue to operate as they now do, the earth, after an indefinite time, must be burned with fire.		It is another curious circumstance also to be noted, that an old fisherman living on the banks of the Sea of Galilee saw the same fact, (2 Pet. iii., 7).		"The heavens and the earth are reserved unto fire."		They pass away in their present form.

Our earth is now burned up.		It has fulfilled its purpose.		We may look back upon the scenes which it has presented : scenes for epics, for comedy, and for tragedy ; of heroic deeds, and of cowardly deeds ; of lofty purposes, and base purposes ; of joys and sorrows ; of bright prospects, and dark disappointments ; of smiles and of tears running down the furrows made by them ; of buoyant strength, and wasting disease ; of blooming health, and of wounds and blood ; of friendships and strifes ; of peace and war ; of the plough calling forth the riches of the soil, and the sword drenching it with blood ; of happy and peaceful families, of distracted families and desolate households ; There is the mother rejoicing over her new-born babe, and Rachel weeping for her children, and refusing to be comforted ; there is the lover's love, the wife's devotion, and the adulterer's lust, separating forever those who would once have died for each other ; there is the patriot dying for his country, and the traitor betraying it to the enemy ; there are the groans of the dying, mingling with the shouts of victory,—all these falling under our observation, narrated in history and biography, pictured in drama and in novels, and experienced here in our own hearts and lives.

This is the scene presented in the First Epoch ; but this is not to be the Last Epoch. Were it so, we should feel it to be unworthy of God. But we have evidence that he all along purposed something better, and prepared for it. There has been a battle leading to victory and unending peace. There has been a winter with its storms, but the winter is over and gone, and is succeeded by eternal spring. There has been night lighted only by stars,

but the evening is followed by morning, and
the evening and morning constitute the seventh
day.

At the close the earth perishes. Having
been the scene of so much sin, it is fit that it
should be purified by fire. "The heavens
shall pass away with a great noise, and the elements shall melt with fervent heat, and the
earth also, and the works that are therein shall
be burned up." The tares and the wheat have
grown together until the harvest, but now the
tares are burned up and the wheat is gathered
into the garner. The evil is separated forever,
and all that is good remains in the day when
God maketh up his jewels.

I cherish the belief that each of God's innumerable worlds may have its own manifestation
of the glory of God, each star differing from
another in glory. "There is one glory of the
sun and another glory of the moon and another
glory of the stars." We know what the glory
of our world is. It may not have been equalled,
it cannot be surpassed, by the glory of any
other. A derangement has occurred. "By
one man sin entered into the world, and death
by sin." But "when sin abounded grace did
much more abound." Sin is condemned, and

yet the sinner is saved. The Logos becomes flesh and dwelt among us ; the Creator and Creature are brought into closest relationship. But the end to be accomplished by the God-Man's kingdom is now accomplished. "When all things shall be subdued unto him, then shall the Son also himself be subject unto him that put all things under him, that God may be all in all" (I Cor. xv., 28). I can see no farther into the endless light that stretches out beyond. My hope is to be there and live there forever ; then shall I know, even as also I am known.

THE END.

For EU product safety concerns, contact us at Calle de José Abascal, 56–1°,
28003 Madrid, Spain or eugpsr@cambridge.org.

www.ingramcontent.com/pod-product-compliance
Ingram Content Group UK Ltd.
Pitfield, Milton Keynes, MK11 3LW, UK
UKHW012338130625
459647UK00009B/374